THE BRAZILIAN-PORTUGUESE SLANG PHRASEBOOK

THE BRAZILIAN-PORTUGUESE SLANG PHRASEBOOK

The Ultimate Soccer Fan's Guide to Slang, Music, Fun, and *Futebol*

ALICE ROSE, NATI VALE, AND JADSON CAÇADOR

Formerly published as *Party Brazil Phrasebook 2014*

Published by:
Ulysses Press
PO Box 3440
Berkeley, CA 94703
www.ulyssespress.com

ISBN: 978-1-64604-591-4
Library of Congress Control Number: 2023946393

Printed in the United States
10 9 8 7 6 5 4 3 2 1

Interior artwork: see page 150
Editors: Claire Chun, Yesenia Garcia-Lopez, Renee Rutledge

To the people of Brazil that can party like no others on this planet.
After all, "quem não gosta de samba, bom sujeito não é ..."

Contents

USING THIS BOOK

This book should help you pick up enough Portuguese phrases to make you sound and act like a local in any situation—from the beaches to the nightclubs and the restaurants to the shops.

This phrasebook is no Portuguese 101—it's not designed to be your only resource for the language. What it will do is help you save face in Brazil. Use it to enhance your experience with the latest *futebol* terms, witty responses, and sexy pickup lines. Each English word or phrase is followed by its Portuguese equivalent. Study the words carefully and use them wisely. This primer could very well earn you some local *amigos* or even help you avoid a fistfight. At the very least, it should stop you from looking like an ignorant tourist.

Quick and Dirty Portuguese Pronunciation

Portuguese is phonetic, so it won't take you long to pronounce unfamiliar words on your own. Here are some basics to get you started.

Vowels

Don't be alarmed by all the accents. There are four different kinds and they always follow the same rules. Usually the second-to-last syllable in a word is automatically stressed, so when there is an acute accent (´) on a vowel, it just means the word is stressed on that syllable instead. If an acute accent is at the end of a word, it has an open sound (*café*: ka-FÉ; coffee). The little hat, or circumflex accent (^) expresses a closed sound (*você*: vo-SÊ; like the vowel sound in "say"). A grave accent (`) doesn't change the sound of the word; it's just used for contractions. A tilde (~) nasalizes the vowel sound (as if you are congested) (*alemã*: a-le-MÃ; like the vowel sound in "rang"). Vowels before a syllable ending with an "m" or an "n" that are followed by another consonant are also nasalized, as in the words *falam* (they speak) and *quando* (when). Some vowels change sound when they're at the end of a word. A final position "e," as in *lanche* (snack), sounds like the "y" in "baby." A final position "o," like in *livro* (book), sounds like the "oo" in "food."

a	*parte*	like the "a" in "father"
ã	*irmã*	like the "a" in "sang"
e	*ler*	like the "e" in "bet"
ê	*português*	like the "e" in "they"
i	*comida*	like the "i" in "machine"
o	*nova*	like the "a" in "law"
ô	*avô*	like "oh"
u (stressed)	*luz*	like the "oo" in "too"
u (unstressed)	*mulher*	like the "u" in "bull"; the sound is almost nasal

Consonants

Consonants are generally pronounced like they are in English, with a few exceptions. There are two consonant pairs that you will never find in English: "lh," pronounced like the "lli" in "million" (*filha*: fi-LIA; daughter) and "nh," pronounced like the "ni" in "onion" (*vinho*: vi-NIO; wine). The cedilla (ç) is another distinctive consonant that is pronounced like a soft "s" where a "c" would normally represent a hard sound "k" (*coração*: ko-ra-SAO; heart).

> c sounds like the "s" in "sad" before "e" and "i": *cedo* (SE-du; early), *cima* (SI-ma; top). But it sounds like the "c" in "cake" before "a," "o," or "u": *cama* (KA-ma; bed), *coisa* (KOI-sa; thing), *curtir* (KUR-tir; to enjoy).
>
> ch sounds like the English "sh" in "shower": *achar* (a-SHAR; to think/believe).
>
> d is usually pronounced like the "g" in "gee-whiz" before "e" and "i": *saúde* (sa-U-ge; health), *dia* (GI-a; day).
>
> h is silent at the beginning of a word: *hoje* (O-je; today).
>
> j The "j" in Portuguese, like in Rio de Janeiro, is softer than it is in English, but it's not at all like it sounds in Spanish.
>
> l after a vowel tends to become a "w" sound like in "few": *Brasil* (Brah-ZEW).
>
> r at the beginning of a word and "rr" in the middle of a word are pronounced like an English "h": Rio de Janeiro (HE-o ge ja-NEI-ru), *carro* (KA-hu; car).
>
> s at the beginning of a word or after a consonant and a double "ss" sounds like the "s" in "seat": *sol* (SO; sun), *conseguir* (kon-SE-gir; to obtain), *osso* (O-so; bone). But "s" sounds like the "z" in "zoo" between two vowels: *casa* (KA-za; house). In some parts of Brazil, the "s" can sound like the "sh" in "shower" at the end of a word

or before "c," "f," "p," "q," or "t": *palavras* (pa-la-VRASH; words), *gostar* (gosh- TAR; to like).

t is usually pronounced like the "ch" in "cheer" before "e" and "i": *noite* (NOI-chi; night), *tio* (CHI-o; uncle).

x sounds like the "sh" in "shower" at the beginning of a word, before a consonant, and sometimes before two vowels: *xarope* (sha-RO-pe; syrup). But it sounds like the "s" in "sun" between two vowels: *próximo* (PRO-si-mo; next). It can also sound like the "z" in "zoo" when "ex" is before a vowel: *exame* (e-ZA-me; test).

Nasal consonants, "**m**" and "**n**," are pronounced through the nose, not the mouth. Hence the name. "M" is nasalized when it's at the end of a syllable after a vowel, so it sounds like the "m" in "him": *combater* (kom-ba-TER; to fight). At the end of a word, "m" is barely pronounced: *sim* (SEE; yes). "N" is nasalized when it comes at the end of a syllable after a vowel and before a consonant, so it sounds like the "ng" in "sing": *sensível* (seng-SI-vew; sensitive).

Stress

Stress typically falls on the next-to-last syllable, except for words ending in "i," "u," diphthongs, consonants, and nasal vowels. These words carry the stress in the last syllable. All other changes in stress require the use of a written accent, which gives a visual clue as to where to place the emphasis.

Rhythm, Cadence, and Regional Accents

Just like the rest of the world, where you live—and how much money you have—shapes the way you speak. However, one speech trait most Portuguese speakers do share is the tendency to shorten or jam words together. This is done in different ways, from simple abbreviations (i.e., *para* becomes *pra*, *estou* becomes *tô*, and *está* becomes *tá*) to entire phrases

(*Olhe para aí*, or "Oh, would you look at that," becomes *Ó paí ó* (Ohpah-EE Oh). Articulation is subtle, so be careful not to overpronunciate. Foreigners usually sound idiotic because they attempt to enunciate e-ve-ry syllable. Loosen up your tongue and remember that Portuguese is not Spanish! A lot of the words and structures may be very similar but pay attention to the differences — you do, after all, want to blend in with the locals. Whether you're off to Belo Horizonte, Manaus, or Rio de Janeiro, try to pick up on the way they do things there; it will certainly make your stay more fulfilling. *Boa viagem*!

CHAPTER 1

WELCOME TO BRAZIL

Bem Vindo ao Brasil

Ranked as the fifth largest country in the world, Brazil's economy is the largest in Latin America. A number of the FIFA host cities are situated along its impressive Atlantic coastline, and each one has its own distinct flavor, adding to the country's great diversity. We encourage you to take some time to delve deeper into the history, culture, and natural wonders each urban core has to offer. We'll give you a quick overview of each city but first, *futebol*.

★★★ Brazilian Soccer
Futebol Brasileiro

Carnaval, "The Girl from Ipanema," or the Amazon rainforest and its tropical birds may all come to mind when you think of Brazil, but what stands out foremost is *futebol*. Soccer is engrained in the life of every *brasileiro*; everything in the country revolves around this glorious game. Every kid dreams about being a soccer player; every adult wants their son to be one; and every grandparent is disappointed that their son wasn't one. On the beach, on the grass, in the street, in the park, you'll see kids and adults playing soccer everywhere. It's in their blood, it's in the curve of their feet, and it's in their soul.

Where does all of this passion come from? How did Brazilians get so damn good at playing the beautiful game? Read on to better understand why Brazilians are so crazy for soccer.

Beautiful Game
Jogo Bonito

If you have a little knowledge of soccer you have probably heard the expression "the beautiful game" (*jogo bonito*) or as Brazilians say, *futebol arte* (literally, "football art"). *Futebol arte* encapsulates the swag, the *ginga* (swing), and the innate improvisational skills Brazilians possess when they play the game. Some people claim it has been disappearing over the last few years, but Brazilians don't think so—they know that their fluid style of play differentiates them from the rest of the "soccer world." Perhaps it is an extension of the samba culture, but Brazil has such a graceful, flowing game, it's as if they are dancing with the ball.

The Beginning
O Início

Charles Miller popularized the game in Brazil at the end of the 19th century when he brought soccer equipment and a rule book from England (the sport's birthplace) to São Paulo and taught his friends how to play. Miller also organized exhibition matches in affluent São Paulo. By the beginning of the 20th century, a number of clubs and leagues were created here and in nearby Rio de Janeiro, which at that time was the capital city of Brazil. These two cities began holding soccer tournaments as an extension of their historic rivalry, and soon, soccer leagues spread north and eventually nationwide.

A National Identity
Identidade Nacional

The soccer leagues were initially established for the white elite, but African-Brazilian players began to show up on team rosters. In 1912 many of the larger and more influential league teams tried to surreptitiously ban all black players by creating another all-white league that excluded any club that had black players. This racially driven move failed within a year, opening the door for teams to hire the best player, no matter what race.

The predominately black and native working class loved soccer too, and began to organize casual games among themselves wherever they could play. They didn't need fancy stadiums, just a ball, a flat field, and their incredible passion, which is just as intense today as it was all these years ago.

By the time the first World Cup was held in 1930, Brazil was poised to dominate the international soccer arena. Soccer's popularity had crossed race and class lines, embedding the sport into the country's national identity. *Futebol* was no longer just for well-to-do Europeans but a sport all *brasileiros* embraced as their own.

World Cups
Copas do Mundo

With *futebol* such a visceral part of Brazil, it's no wonder that the Brazilian National Team is the only squad in the world that has participated in every World Cup since its inception in 1930. Brazil has also made it to the finals the most (seven times) and, of course, has won the most titles (1958, 1962, 1970, 1994, 2002).

The 1958 World Cup was a defining moment in Brazilian soccer history. Headed by the great Pelé, the Brazilian national soccer team outshone the Swedes in the championship match to clinch Brazil's first World Cup with a number of records, including youngest player to participate in a World Cup final (Pelé, who was 17) and the highest number of goals scored by a winning team (five goals). Pelé, a hero to his country and adored by all, led Brazil to two more World Cup wins with the help of other great players like Garrincha, Didi, and Zagallo.

Despite the trophies, Brazil's national team continues to be consistently strong and one of the teams always favored to win the World Cup and other international competitions.

Players
Jogadores

Brazilian players have always had something special when it comes to the playing field—fantastic ball control, quick thinking, and the capacity to improvise are hallmarks of the top footballers. Here is a very short list of some of history's greatest and how much they have impacted the game.

Pelé: With more than 1,000 career goals, Pelé is a national icon. Also known as *O Rei* (The King) he was the star of Santos, a professional club team. After an unprecedented three World Cup wins in 1958, 1962, and 1970, he became internationally recognized and adored, and is arguably (not by Brazilians, obviously) the greatest soccer player of all time. In 2000 FIFA elected Pelé best soccer player of the century.

Romário: Romário, known as *Baixinho* (Shorty) because of his small stature (5'6"), was one of soccer's greatest strikers. He was elected player of the year in 1994 and was pivotal in the campaign to bring the World Cup to Brazil that same year. While he played in the Netherlands and Spain (Barcelona), he spent most of his career in Brazil. Romário has a strong personality and when still playing used to defiantly say, "Why should I train if I know what I am supposed to do?" And he really did know it. He also scored more than 1,000 career goals according to his own count (although some people are skeptical of this).

Ronaldo: Elected player of the year three times, Ronaldo won two World Cups and is currently the player that has scored the most cumulative goals in World Cup history. He struggled with serious injuries during his career but always came back and even today he is a symbol of Brazilian *superação* (overcoming). Also known as *O Fenômeno* (The Phenomenon), Ronaldo was a CF (central forward) like no one had ever seen before. His talent and speed were a rarity in soccer, and combined with an incredible facility to strike made Ronaldo one of the greatest footballers of all time.

Ronaldinho: Ronaldinho was at the peak of his career from 2004 to 2006; he was elected player of the year in both 2004 and 2005, and also won the 2002 World Cup. With a large repertory of goals and dribbles, an always-smiling Ronaldinho made an already beautiful game into something magical. When playing offense, he would leave his opponents in the dust after deftly dribbling past them. He was Barcelona and Brazil's number 10 and led both to great glories. With the national team,

Ronaldinho never performed quite like he did in Barcelona, but there's no doubt his game represents the *futebol arte* characteristic of Brazilian soccer.

 Cities
Cidades

We'll let your travel guidebooks lead you to the best accommodations and restaurants, but here is a brief synopsis of popular cities to visit.

Manaus

Manaus, or the metropolis of the Amazon, is one of Brazil's ten largest cities. Situated on the mouth of the Amazon River, its location makes the city an ideal base to explore the nearby rainforest by boat. Despite its proximity to the jungle, don't be fooled—Manaus is a large, modern city that became an economic powerhouse in the 1960s after the construction of the Manaus Industrial Pole, an area where generous federal tax breaks attracted businesses that consequently could offer goods to the public at lower prices.

With its proximity to the river, fish is prominent in local cuisine. Both the *tambaqui* (part of the piranha family) and *tucunaré* (a type of bass) are especially good grilled.

Some must-see places: the **Teatro Amazonas,** one of the most important neoclassical monuments in Brazil, and the **Encontro das Águas,** the confluence of the Rio Negro ("dark-colored waters") and Rio Solimões ("muddy waters").

Bars don't stay open late in central Manaus. Your best bet for a night scene is the **Ponta Negra** beach area.

Fortaleza

Heading to the northeast, the state of Ceará boasts Fortaleza, the fifth largest (and most densely populated) city in Brazil. This coastal city with dune-laden beaches is great for basking in the sun but less than ideal for swimming — the water tends to be polluted in many areas. But if you are itching to take a dip, check out **Praia do Futuro** (be forewarned — the waves are rough).

The most famous landmark in the city is **Nossa Senhora da Assunção**, a fort that was built by the Dutch in the 1800s. There is a nice boardwalk in **Meireles** and an over-the-top, raging nightlife in the district of **Iracema**, dotted with restaurants, bars, and clubs.

The food is eclectic — ranging from sushi, Italian, and *churrasco* (Brazilian barbecue). But if you want to taste the regional favorites look for *muqueca* (seafood stew) and *carangueijo* (crab). If you're more interested in a country-style night out, head over to **Avenida Beira Mar** for some *forró* dancing.

Natal

Named for the day the city was founded in 1599, Natal, or "Christmas," is the picture-perfect capital of Rio Grande do Norte. It's one of the nicest beach destinations in Brazil thanks to its endless rolling sand dunes and tropical coral reefs just offshore. The city itself is fairly small, compared to other Brazilian metropolises, and you can walk around most of it (although some areas can get sketchy, so ask around about unsafe areas or skip the walking and take a taxi if you're not sure).

You can also catch a bus to **Ponta Negra** in the southern part of the city, which is the spot to chill if you're looking for a day of sunbathing and people-watching — it's essentially the Venice Beach of South America, with a happening urban scene and plenty of artsy types romping around. Or rent a dune buggy here and visit the beaches lining the coast. In

BRASIL

World Cup Stadiums

Arena Amazônia (Vivaldão)
Manaus, Amazonas

Estádio Governador Plácido Castelo (Castelão)
Fortaleza, Ceará

Arena das Dunas (Machadão)
Natal, Rio Grande do Norte

Itaipava Arena Pernambuco
Recife, Pernambuco

Itaipava Arena Fonte Nova (Fonte Nova)
Salvador, Bahia

Arena Pantanal (Verdão)
Cuiabá, Mato Grosso

Estádio Nacional de Brasília Mané Garrincha (Estádio Nacional)
Brasília, Brasília DF

Estádio Governador Magalhães Pinto (Mineirão)
Belo Horizonte, Minas Gerais

Estádio Jornalista Mário Filho (Maracanã)
Rio de Janeiro, Rio de Janeiro

Arena São Paulo (Itaquerão)
São Paulo, São Paulo

Estádio Joaquim Américo Guimarães (Arena da Baixada)
Curitiba, Paraná

Estádio José Pinheiro Borda (Beira-Rio)
Porto Alegre, Rio Grande do Sul

Maracajaú (63km from Natal), the largest cluster of offshore reefs in the country attracts snorkelers and scuba divers. Swimming is best at **Praia da Pipa** or **Praia do Cento,** where the water is not polluted like the beaches in Natal proper. There are also *barracas* that serve beer and delicious fresh fried fish, often accompanied by live music.

If the beach isn't your thing, visit Natal's **Forte dos Reis Magos,** the most recognized monument in town. Or treat yourself to the plentiful shopping and good eats in Natal City.

Ponta Negra definitely has the liveliest nightlife in the area. Visit the bars that line the streets and enjoy live music. After you've bar-hopped your way through the early evening, head to the clubs, which don't open until around midnight.

For some cultural flavor, check out the **Festas Juninas** (page 94), an annual June celebration Natal is famous for.

Recife

Recife, "rocky reefs" in Portuguese, is named for the coral barrier that sits 200 meters offshore. Dutch architecture is vibrantly sprinkled through the city—a vestige of Holland's colonization. The nearby city of **Olinda,** with its brightly painted colonial buildings and cobblestone streets, is an especially fine example of this European influence (so much so that it's a UNESCO World Heritage Site). There are a number of historical monuments and plazas around the two cities so history buffs—go wild! **Recife Antigo** (Old Recife) is the state of Pernambuco's old port where sugar cane was transported to Portugal. A Jewish community in Recife that settled during the Dutch occupation is still prominent there today.

Nightlife centers around **Recife Antigo; Rua Bom Jesus** (formerly Rua dos Judeus or "Street of the Jews") has a plethora of bars, restaurants, and streets packed with revelers. For a calmer evening, head to **Patio São Pedro** in Santo Antônio.

While Recife hosts Brazil's third largest Carnaval, you won't see Rio's glamorous parade or Salvador's gritty street parties (page 93). The vibe is much more traditional, honoring its cultural past with tireless energy and enthusiasm. Performers parade through the streets in colorful outfits and dance to the upbeat sounds of *frevo* (page 98).

For water play, head to **Porto de Galinhas** where there's snorkeling and scuba diving. **Maracaípe** and **Praia de Boa Viagem** are nice beach spots but swimming is prohibited due to numerous shark attacks in the past.

Just like any major city, Recife has its downfalls with awful traffic, noise, crime, and stench (from the pollution). Driving is not recommended, but Recife has a decent metro system, and buses and taxis are readily available.

Salvador

One of Brazil's first cities and its first capital, Salvador is rich with history and culture. Throughout the 16th and 17th centuries it was the nucleus of sugar production and one of South America's main centers for the slave trade. Salvador's strong African-Brazilian heritage is reflected in the city's music, dance, religion and food, all heavily influenced by its oppressed past. **Pelourinho**, a UNESCO World Heritage Site, is the historic core of the city. Here you'll find small museums and beautiful churches such as **Igreja de São Francisco**, which has elaborate gold-leaf details and Portuguese blue tiles, and **Igreja da Nossa Senhora do Rosário dos Pretos**, which has a small cemetery in the back where slaves were once buried. There are many capoeira and dance schools in the neighborhood, where you can take a class or see a performance. Salvador and its surrounding cities are the birthplace of samba and many other musical genres such as *axé* and samba-reggae. Another iconic structure in Salvador is the **Elevador Lacerda**, the world's first urban elevator and formerly the world's tallest. It takes you from the upper to the lower city, where you can visit the **Mercado Modelo** where during the slave era, Africans were taken directly off the boats and held until their auction. Now it's a huge indoor market where tourists can buy *lembranças da Bahia* (souvenirs).

There is plenty going on in the **Pelourinho** at night, with live music, outdoor bars, and restaurants serving authentic *comida baiana*. While you are there make sure to try *acarajé* (a street food made from fried bean paste and stuffed with tomatoes, shrimp, and okra) or the *muqueca*, a seafood stew cooked in coconut milk and *dendê* oil (a bright yellow palm oil).

An authentic beach scene isn't very far away — **Porto da Barra** and **Barra Vento** are the city's most crowded beaches. If you want something a bit more secluded, hop on an air-conditioned mini bus to **Litoral Norte**. Depending on the time of day, it could take anywhere from 40 minutes to 2 hours from the city center. You can also take the ferry across the bay to **Itaparica Island** for a nice view of the city.

Buses and taxis are the best way to get around Salvador.

Cuiabá

Moving to the central-western region of Brazil, Cuiabá sits in the dead center of South America. It also happens to be one of the hottest (temperature-wise) cities in the country. With the modern expansion of federal roadways into Mato Grosso, this capital city continues its rapid growth that began with gold in 1719 and later agriculture. Ecotourism plays a part in the city's current economy. Cuiabá is located at the base of the Amazon, the **Pantanal** (tropical wetlands rich with wildlife), and the foot of the **Chapada dos Guimarães** mountain range. Nature-loving footballers, this is your spot. The city has a few museums like the **Museu do Marechal Rondon**, which displays Native American artifacts.

What nightlife there is centers around the **Praça Popular** (formally, Praça Eurico Gaspar Dutra) and **Avenida Getúlio**. Starting the first week of July is the month-long **Festa de São Benedito**, a grand celebration of

Saint Benedict, the namesake for **Igreja Nossa Senhora do Rosário e Capela de São Benedito.**

Brasília

Brasília, the capital of Brazil, is a relative baby compared to the country's other colonial cities. The city, the fourth largest in Brazil, did not exist prior to 1956, when then president Juscelino Kubitchek ordered its construction. Brazilian Oscar Niemeyer, a world-class architect, and Lucio Costa, a renowned urban planner, were enlisted to plan and develop the city. A bird's-eye view reveals that Brasília is shaped like an airplane, an innovation in design that earned the city a spot on the UNESCO's World Heritage List. Make sure to check out the **Praça dos Três Poderes,** a town square that gets its name from its location in between the three federal branches; the **Catedral Metropolitana,** the first monument built in Brasília which was designed by Niemeyer as a hyperboloid structure with 16 columns, weighing 90 tons each; and the **TV Tower,** the highest point in the city, with a 75-meter-high observation deck, and the second-best place (after a helicopter) to appreciate the city's beautiful design.

To get around, take a taxi or rent a car, but be forewarned that traffic can be terrible.

Belo Horizonte

Southeastern Brazil's Belo Horizonte, or "Beautiful Horizon," is known for providing the best quality of life. This precisely planned city is a bustling metropolis dotted with parks, but *paulistas* and *cariocas* (resident from the larger cities of São Paulo and Rio) still consider it a farm town. BH (pronounced "Beagá") is not generally a tourist destination, but is a draw for those interested in modern architecture and urban design. Belo Horizonte is the first Brazilian city with a railroad system and overall, public transportation runs smoothly (which is good because the driving is a bit crazy!). Everything in the downtown area is walkable, but you should take cabs at night. For great shopping head to **Barro Preto,** Belo Horizonte's garment district, where you'll find tradition with a modern twist. Beautifully crafted items handmade by *caipiras* (local country folk) are for sale at the **Feira de Artes e Artesanatos,** one of the biggest flea markets in Latin America. Some of the *comida mineira* (local farm-style food with African and indigenous influences) to try are local cheeses like *queijo minas* and the delicious *pão de queijo* (cheese bread). But it's not only simple farm-style food that's available. Belo Horizonte is known for its fine gastronomy and array of international cuisine. The best bars and cafes are in the *Centro Sul* area but be aware that a lot of the upscale clubs have consumption minimums, so it might get pricey if you plan on bar-hopping.

Rio de Janeiro

A cidade maravilhosa or "marvelous city," as the song goes, does not do Rio justice. With some of the most breathtaking views, Rio is one of the world's most glamorous cities. Located at the foot of Guanabara Bay, the city is home to some of Brazil's most iconic sites: **Corcovado** (the mountain with Christ perched atop, watching over the entire city), **Pão de Açúcar** (a popular mountain where you can take a gondola ride up to the top), the **Sambódromo** (where Rio's unique Carnaval parade occurs), and of course the expanse of beaches including **Copacabana** and **Ipanema.** Other popular destinations are the **Jardim Botânico** (Botanical Garden) and the trolley up to **Santa Teresa** (a quaint neighborhood with stellar city views).

A number of new, hip restaurants are clustered in the **Leblon** neighborhood, but good eats are also sprinkled throughout the city.

For beach lounging, head to **Copacabana** (not for swimming though), **Ipanema,** or the more upscale **Leblon. Barra de Tijuca,** the Miami of Brazil, is great for surfing as well as swimming and sunning.

Rio is the samba hub of the world and the birthplace of bossa nova, a slower, jazzier version of samba. Live music, bars, and clubs—the city sizzles with the hottest parties in the country. **Ipanema** has plenty of small bars and music clubs. Head to **Lapa** for an even livelier scene. If you're looking for something a bit more "red," **Copacabana** can feed your needs.

Rio is an enormous city with an expansive bus system and decent bike paths. Rent a two-wheeler or ask around about buses, otherwise taxis are the best option. Keep in mind that it isn't safe to bicycle at night, however.

São Paulo

São Paulo or Sampa, as it's known to locals, is the third largest city in the world (population is about 11 million). With lineages from Portugal, Italy, Japan, Africa, and the Netherlands (to name a few), the city is the most ethnically diverse in all of Brazil and *paulistanos* are very proud of these international roots. The city has a reputation for being one of the world's ugliest cities and is nicknamed Terra da Garoa (the Land of the Drizzle), after its renowned weather instability and plentiful rainfall. Sampa is not really a touristy city to "see," it is a city to "be in."

The two main draws for visitors are food and business, but the **Mercado Municipal**, **Parque Ibirapuera**, and **Banespa Building** (with great city views) are worth checking out.

The best restaurants are located in the **Jardins** area, an upscale, high-rise district; for great Japanese food, there's **Liberdade**, a neighborhood like Los Angeles's Little Tokyo or San Francisco's Japantown.

For a night out head to **Vila Madalena** (which has a slightly hippie style) or **Itaím Bibi**.

Getting around is relatively easy. The **Metrô** is recognized as one of the best in the world: fast, clean, and safe.

The Hood
Favela

If you're interested in getting to know a city beyond the superficial tourist areas, visit the *favelas*. This is where the heart and soul of the culture is: where the music is born, where the best soccer players grow up, and where you'll have authentic encounters with the locals. Whether you want to play a pickup game with some kids, practice capoeira, or go to a *baile funk*, the *favelas* always have a lot going on.

This is not to say you should wander into any *favela* without a care in the world. In fact, these are the most dangerous places in the big cities and you can get in very, very serious trouble there. Most of the *favelas* are run by drug lords and being there alone can put your life in danger. That being said, not everyone who lives in a *favela* is a criminal; most people living there are ordinary hard-working citizens. So if you want to get a flavor of the *favela*, go with someone you trust and who knows the neighborhood well.

Curitiba

The influx of Germans, Italians, Ukrainians, and Poles in the 19th century created a cultural richness in Curitiba, the most populous city in southern Brazil. The city is recognized worldwide as a model in dealing with transportation and environmental issues; it's especially well-known for its wonderful bus system. The downtown area is very walkable, though you'll want to catch a taxi if you're canvassing the city from corner to corner.

Though not known as a party town, there are two centers of night activity: the historic center's **Largo da Ordem** and the **Betel** neighborhood.

Be sure to check out the pedestrian marketplace **Rua das Flores** (or **Calçadão** as it's known locally); the **Rua 24 Horas**, a collection of restaurants, bars, and shops open 24/7 (great for late-night snacks); and the **Centro Histórico**.

Porto Alegre

Porto Alegre is the biggest urban mass in southern Brazil, and a top cultural, political, and economic center. This wealthy Latin American city's strong European heritage pairs well with its subtropical climate. Known to other Brazilians as *gaúcho* country and the "Mercosul capital," Porto Alegre is currently the largest port city in Brazil. It has the country's highest quality of life rating along with very progressive politics.

The metro and buses are quite reliable when moving around the city, and within the downtown area everything is only a 15-minute walk away. If you are a big meat-eater, indulge yourself with some *churrasco gaúcho*. Brazil is known for its delicious grilled meats, especially in Rio Grande do Sul. Don't leave without visiting the **Mercado Público**, a public market housed in an 1869 neoclassical building that was completely restored in the 1990s.

★★★ Dos and Don'ts
Certo e Errado

While these are some pretty standard rules of travel, some are specific to Brazil. We want you to be safe so you can enjoy your trip to the fullest. Just be aware that you are nowhere near home in terms of location, culture, and manners. Be on your best behavior and try to be aware of everything around you.

General
Em Geral

☆ Be aware of your surroundings. If there aren't a lot of people around, it means you are more vulnerable to anyone who could be lurking around the corner.

☆ Don't walk around with a bunch of credit cards or your passport (but always have some form of identification on you) or jewelry.

☆ Don't be scared if people randomly approach you and start talking. Brazilians are more congenial with strangers than Americans are.

☆ If you have to carry a purse, make it one that isn't easy to yank off your shoulder.

☆ Don't carry a water bottle. You will stick out like a sore thumb. Be like the local and buy ice-cold water from vendors that are all over the place.

☆ Don't wear anything flashy. Your blinging watch, ring, or even tennis shoes make you a target. (Brazilians can always tell a tourist by their shoes.) Especially sandals with socks—a huge no-no.

☆ Brazilians love to help people. They will direct you or sometimes even take you to the destination you are looking for. Look to vendors, police officers, and people that you can tell are in the area all the time.

☆ Don't use your iPhone, iPad, or other mobile device out and about in blithe ignorance. Just because you see the locals doing it doesn't mean you can do the same.

☆ Don't throw toilet paper in the toilet bowl. Simply: You will clog the toilet.

☆ Don't dress down when you're at the mall. So no sandy-footed flip-flops post-beach, but a nice clean T-shirt will do just fine.

☆ Listen to some live music (samba, *forró*... whatever your heart desires).

☆ When at a restaurant, ask about how small (or big) a portion you want before your order. If you don't specify, they will you bring the biggest and charge you more.

☆ Don't plan too much. Go with the flow, but be smart about it.

On the Street
Na Rua

☆ Don't be afraid to ask the locals whether it's a good idea to go somewhere, especially in the big cities.

☆ When asking for directions, don't take the first person's word for it. Thank them and then ask a second person to confirm.

☆ Be watchful, not only of your surroundings, but of how locals do things. If they flag the bus down by pointing their finger to the ground, don't wave your hand in the air like you're hailing a taxi in NYC. If they enter through the back of the bus — you should too.

☆ Wait for the light and the cars to stop to cross the street. Pedestrians do not have the right of way and cars will not stop for you. No joke.

☆ Take public transportation whenever possible.

At the Beach
Na Praia

☆ Leave your American swimsuit at home. Don't be shy and buy a sexy Brazilian bikini! Guys, you may think you are cool with your board shorts but in Brazil, even the men show their skin. It's time to whip out your Speedo.

☆ No need to smuggle the hotel towels to the beach. Grab a *canga* (sarong). It fits a lot easier in your bag and it dries much faster. No one brings towels to the beach.

☆ If locals won't swim there, DON'T SWIM THERE! The water is probably polluted or the waves are too rough.

☆ Bring your own sunscreen. Not only is the sun extremely hot, a lot of the people who sell sunscreen on the beach tend to water it down and charge more.

☆ Obey the signs. If a sign says not to get in the water because there are shark attacks, it doesn't mean one time someone saw a shark—it means shark attacks have happened on multiple occasions so you should stay clear of the water.

THE BASICS
O Básico

You did it! You're in Brazil! So you're a little jet-lagged... that's fine, you're tough, you can sleep when it's over. Let the adrenaline kick in and enjoy the ride.

★★★ Hello
Olá

Like every other language, Portuguese has a ton of ways to meet and greet. Know your audience. Need to ask the immigration officer to rubber stamp your passport? Keep it formal. Same goes for anyone significantly older than you or people you meet in a semiformal situation. But it's fine to be less formal when chatting with friends your age or in a casual setting like a bar or a pickup soccer game.

It's best to keep your greetings formal until you've gotten to know the person you're talking to.

Hello.
Olá.

How are you?
Como vai o senhor / a senhora?

Good morning.
Bom dia.

Good afternoon.
Boa tarde.

Good evening/night.
Boa noite.

Hanging out with your friends at the local bar or crashing a party to meet new people? Skip the fancy talk and keep the tone informal.

Hi.
Oi.

Hey man, **what's up**?
*Iaí cara, **tudo bom?***

It's all good.
Tudo bem.
Tudo bem can also mean "Hello," "How are you?" or even "What's up?" when used as a greeting.

Afternoon/Evening
Boa.

How are ya?
Como vai você?

How you doing?
Como você tá?

What's good?
Diga aí.

What's new?
Quais são as novidades?

What are you up to?
O que você manda?

What's going on?
Qualé?
Short for *qual é.*

What's happening, man?
***Que foi**, rapaz?*
Literally, "What went?"

What's up, bro?
Iaí, bro?

What's the word?
Qualé menor?

How you doing?
Como você tá?

Sometimes you're up, sometimes you're down. Such is life, especially when it comes to sports. That said, please try to keep your Debbie Downer comments to a minimum. We're trying to have fun here!

What are you doing?
O que você tá fazendo?

Whatcha up to, fool?
O que tá pegando, sacana?

What's going down?
O que tá rolando?

What's good?
Qual é a boa?

It's been a while since I've seen you.
Tem um tempão que não te vejo.

Where've you been?!
Cadê você?!
Literally, "Where are you?"

You've been M.I.A.!
Você sumiu!
Literally, "You disappeared."

I'm good.
Na boa.

It's all good.
Beleza.

Okay.
Okay. | É nós.

I can't complain.
Só alegria.
Literally, "only happiness."

Everything's...
Tudo...

> good.
> *na boa.*
>
> all right.
> *certo.*
>
> joyful.
> *jóia.*
>
> at peace.
> *em paz.*

I'm in a bad mood.
Tô de mau humor.

Things are pretty messed up.
Tá tudo de cabeça pra baixo.

Hanging in there.
Tô na luta.

I've seen better days.
Ja tive dias melhores.

> bad.
> *tá ruim.*
>
> so-so.
> *mais ou menos.*
>
> depressing.
> *tá maus*
>
> stressful.
> *tenso.*

in order.	out of control.
em ordem.	*fora de controle.*
cool.	fucked up.
legal.	*fodido.*

Please, thank you, sorry
Por favor, obrigado, desculpa

Adding some niceties to the end of your phrases is a sure way of showing you're making an effort. It also doesn't hurt to have a quick apology on hand for those foot-in-mouth situations.

Please.
Por favor.

Do me a favor.
Me faz um favor. | Faça o favor.

Thank you.
Obrigado/a. | Brigado/a.
"Thank you" is gender-specific to the speaker, so if you are female, say "*brigada*."

Thanks a lot.
Muito obrigado/a. | Valeu.

You're welcome.
De nada.

No problem.
Imagina. | É nenhuma.

Pardon.
Perdão.

Excuse me.
Com licença. | Licença.

Introducing yourself
Se apresentando

Hi, my name is Chad.
Oi, meu nome é Chad.

I'm American.
Sou americano/a.

What's your name?
Como é seu nome?

I'm Greta.
Meu nome é Greta.

I'm from...
Sou do/da/dos...

> Australia.
> *Austrália.*
>
> Canada.
> *Canadá.*
>
> Denmark.
> *Dinamarca.*
>
> England.
> *Inglaterra.*
>
> France.
> *França.*
>
> Germany.
> *Alemanha.*
>
> Japan.
> *Japão.*
>
> Norway.
> *Noruega.*
>
> Russia.
> *Rússia.*

the Netherlands.
Holanda.

the United States.
Estados Unidos.

I've just arrived in town.
Cheguei agora.

Where's that?
Onde fica?

Are there any around here?
Tem alguma por aqui?

Do you know a good... nearby?
Você sabe onde tem... perto daqui?

> youth hostel
> *um albergue*
>
> bed-and-breakfast
> *uma pousada*
>
> hotel
> *um hotel*

Nice to meet you
Prazer em conhecer você

Pleasure.
Prazer.

Glad to meet you.
Muito prazer.

It was a pleasure.
Foi um prazer.

The pleasure is mine.
O prazer é todo meu.

Likewise.
Igualmente.

What do you do to **kill time**?
*O que você faz pra **passar o tempo**?*

What do you do with your **free time**?
*O que você faz no seu **tempo livre**?*

What do you do?
O que você faz da vida?

Where do you live?
Onde você mora?

Do you live alone?
Você mora sozinho/a?

Can I use your bathroom?
Posso usar o seu banheiro?

Gotta light?
Você tem isqueiro?

★★★ Transportation
Transporte

You'll need to get around somehow. Depending on the city, some modes of transportation are loads better than others. Remember: Not everyone around you is on vacation, so factor in rush-hour traffic when planning your day. If you think NYC is bad at 5:00, you ain't seen nothing. There's no avoiding the traffic (unless you are a super-rich *paulista* who commutes by helicopter).

I'm going to catch/take...
Vou pegar...

> **the bus.**
> ***o ônibus.***
> Buses can be a great way to get around as long as you know where you're going! Don't be afraid to ask the driver or the man taking your money (*o cobrador*). You can also ask someone who is waiting at the bus stop. Brazilians are generally a friendly bunch and will want to help you if they can.

a cab.
um taxi.

There are taxi stands around the main areas of the city and you can also flag them down on the street. Just stick your hand out as they speedily drive by. Taxis run on two different meters: *bandeira 1* during the weekdays and *bandeira 2* on weeknights and weekends. Make sure the driver uses the right one and that they actually use the meter so they don't try to overcharge you.

a van.
uma van.

Officially known as *transporte alternativo* (alternative transportation), these vans generally follow the same line as popular bus routes and cost the same as the stuffy, crowded public option. But while the vans are often air-conditioned and less claustrophobic, they aren't regulated by the city and are potentially dangerous to ride alone. So if you want to try this option, make sure you're with someone who is local and knows the area. Hand your money to the guy at the sliding door and let him know where you want to get off.

Excuse me, where is the **bus stop**?
*Com licença, onde é o **ponto do ônibus**?*

Do you know which bus I take to get to the stadium?
Sabe qual ônibus devo pegar pra ir ao estádio?

You should wait it out. **There is a lot of traffic** right now.
*Deve esperar. **Está tudo engarrafado** agora.*
Traffic is *engarrafamento* or *trafego*.

It's not too far. Let's just take a cab.
Não é muito longe. Vamos de taxi.

Where should I get off?
Onde devo descer?

I'm not sure. Ask the **driver**.
*Não sei. Pergunte ao **motorista**.*

These **cabbies** are crazy drivers!
*Esses **taxistas** dirigem como malucos!*

I've been waiting for the bus for 45 minutes now! Fuck it, I'm walking.
Tô esperando o ônibus há 45 minutos! Caralho, vou a pé.

★★★ Friends
Amigos

Brazilians are friendly, talkative, and like to joke around. Laid-back and liberal, they don't take themselves too seriously, except maybe when it comes to soccer.

How's it hangin', **guys**?
*Tudo bem **pessoal**?*

Where is **everyone**?
*Cadê **todo mundo**?*

The whole **crew** is at the beach.
*A **galera** tá na praia.*

Hey, **peeps**!
*Oi, **gente**!*

What's going on...?
Qualé...?

Sup...?
Fala...

> man
> *rapaz*
>
> homeboy
> *parceiro | camarada*
>
> good guy
> *gente boa*
>
> dude
> *cara*

bro
mano | broder

colleague
colega

boy / girl
menino/a

boyfriend / girlfriend
namorado/a

It's all good, my **brother**.
*Tudo beleza meu **irmão**.*

Where've you been, **girl**?
*Por onde você andava, **menina**?*

No, I don't have a **boyfriend**.
*Não, eu não tenho **namorado**.*

Between you and me
Cá entre nós

Let's be honest, sometimes less is more. The last thing you want to do while standing in line for the bathroom is listen to what the person in front of you feels compelled to share. Use these fillers to keep the conversation going without actually listening.

Uh-huh.
Hurum.

Oh-oh.
Chiii.

Oh, no!
Ai ai ai!

Exactly.
Isso.

Absolutely.
Com certeza.

Agreed.
Falou.

What do you mean?
Como assim?

Got it.
Tô ligado.

For real?
É mesmo?

Beats me.
Sei lá.

So what?
E daí?

I don't care.
E eu com isso?

Never mind.
Deixa pra lá.

Are you serious?
Tá falando sério?

Seriously?
Jura? | Sério?

I can't believe it.
Não acredito.

That's bullshit.
Que besteira.

The Cops
A polícia

If you find yourself in a sticky situation, take a moment to scope out the scene and see if you can spot the police. They'll most likely be an earshot away, especially in tourist areas and sports venues. The police are generally helpful to foreigners but they aren't chummy, so keep it cordial and formal and don't do anything stupid that could get you on their bad side.

Excuse me, officer...
Com licença senhor...

> Can you help me?
> *Pode me ajudar por favor?*
>
> Where is the nearest **ATM**?
> *Onde posso encontrar um **caixa eletrônico** por aqui?*
>
> Can you tell me how to get to the stadium?
> *Como faço pra chegar no estádio?*
>
> **I'm lost** and I don't know the name of my hotel.
> ***Estou perdido** e não sei o nome do meu hotel.*

Ask that **cop** over there.
*Pergunte ao **policial** alí.*

Jesus, there are **cop cars** everywhere.
*Nossa, tem **patrulhas** por todos lados.*

That **MP** was super intimidating.
*Aquele **PM** foi muito intimidador.*

The military police (*polícia militar*) are the city beat cops, so you'll see them everywhere and most often. The city cops (*polícia civil*) function more like detectives who investigate local crimes. And the federal police (*polícia federal*) are just like the U.S. feds—they fight bigger stuff like drug cartel crimes and governmental corruption.

Wow!
Nossa!

Gosh!
Puxa!

Damn!
Droga!

It happens.
Faz parte.

Make do.
Se vira.

Whatever.
Tanto faz.

It's no use.
Não adianta.

I don't give a shit.
Não tô nem aí.

 # Good-bye
Adeus

Bye.
Tchau.

Bye-bye.
Tchauzinho.

See ya.
Até. | Até mais. | Até já.

See you next time.
Até a próxima.

See you soon.
Até logo.

See you tomorrow.
Até amanhã.

I'm going
Já vou

I'm leaving.
Vou embora.

I'm gone.
Fui.

I gotta run.
Vou partir a mil.

It's time to go.
Tá na hora.

I'm...
Tô...

> outta here.
> *caindo fora.*

> out.
> *saindo | indo.*

Stop by anytime.
Apareça.

Stop by more often.
Apareça mais.

Come back soon.
Volte logo.

Come back anytime.
Volte sempre.

Amen!
Amem!

Brazil is a Catholic country, and though a lot of people don't go to church, a lot do. So even when you're having one last drink for the road or leaving a samba club after a raucous night of celebrating your team's victory, your farewells may sound like Sunday High Mass at *Igreja da Penha*. Even if you aren't part of the flock, the proper response for these phrases is *Amem*.

Go with God.
Vai com Deus.

Stay with God.
Fica com Deus.

God bless you.
Deus te abençoe.

God be with you.
Deus te acompanhe.

May God bless you.
Que Deus te abençoe.

You may also get: *Meu pai Oxalá te abençoe* if you're in the North East. Christ is represented by a god named Oxalá, one of the many *orixás* (gods and goddesses) in Candomblé, an Afro-Brazilian polytheistic religion.

May God watch over you.
Que Deus te proteja.

Kisses
Beijos

When it comes to greeting people, you may come across a more affectionate encounter than you are familiar with. Women generally give a little kiss on each cheek if they're friends, and if it's between two guys, usually a casual hand bump or maybe a manly hug. Even when signing off a phone call, you verbally send a kiss before you hang up.

Bye girl, kiss.
Tchau menina, beijo.

Kiss.
Beijo.

Another.
Outro.
This can be a response to *beijo*.

Send a kiss to your mom.
Manda um beijo pra sua mãe.

Big kiss.
Beijão.

Little kiss.
Beijinho.

Smooches.
Beijocas.

CHAPTER 3

SOCCER TALK
Fala Futebol

Let's be real, if you're braving the trip to Brazil during the World Cup, you know your football rules. If you don't—you better Wikipedia it before you leave. However, we bet that the *futebol* talk you know is probably in English mixed with a little Spanish from watching games broadcast on Telemundo (but they talk so fast maybe all you caught was ¡*Goooool*!, which is the same in Portuguese, so you've learned something already!). So we'll brief you on some basic soccer terms in this chapter; info on the actual countries and players is in Chapter 4 (page 63).

★★★ Soccer Terminology
Terminologia do Futebol

Here are some golden vocabulary words for you to throw around when watching the game, reflecting back on it, or joining a pickup game with the locals.

Positions
Posições

He is a good...
Ele é um bom...

> forward.
> *atacante.*
>
> midfielder.
> *meio campo.*
>
> sweeper.
> *lateral.*
>
> defender.
> *zagueiro.*
>
> goalkeeper.
> *goleiro.*
>
> benchwarmer.
> *reserva.*
>
> coach.
> *técnico.*
>
> referee.
> *árbitro.*
>
> ref.
> *juiz.*
>
> ref helper.
> *banderinha.*
> Literally, "little flag."
>
> ball boy.
> *gandula.*
>
> president.
> *presidente.*

Plays
Jogos

That was a...
Foi um...

pass.
passe.

very good pass.
passe com açucar.
Literally, "a sugar pass."

quick pass.
passe na fogueira.
Literally, "bonfire pass." This is when a player receives a pass and his opponent is very close by so he has to be quick in order not to lose possession of the ball.

nutmeg.
caneta.
Passing the ball through the defender's legs.

chip pass.
chapéu. | lençol.
Literally, "hat" or "sheet." It's when someone passes the ball over a defender's head.

pass to yourself.
meia lua. | drible da vaca.
Literally, "half moon" or "cow dribble." This move is like a through pass to oneself; a player kicks the ball to the side of the defender then runs around behind the defender to get the pass.

quick pass.
tabela.
Unlike a *passe na fogueira*, a *tabela* refers to quickly passing the ball between two players.

What a...!
Que...!

> goal
> *gol*

> great goal
> *golaço*

> memorable goal
> *gol de placa*
> A goal that deserves a metal plaque.

> golden goal
> *gol de ouro*

assist
assistência pro gol

> Who gave the **assist**?
> *Quem fez a **assistência pro gol**?*

goal kick
tiro de meta

free kick
cobrança de falta

fake
finta

dribble
ginga | drible

header
cabeçada

sudden death
morte súbita

foul
falta

yellow card
cartão amarelo

penalty
pênalti

red card
cartão vermelho

Locations and time on the field
Locais e tempo no campo

first/second half
primeiro/segundo tempo

field
campo

Pickup games
Peladas

Brazilians play soccer everywhere. A *gringo* shouldn't have a problem joining the group for a quick game, so if you see an informal match happening on the beach, a basketball court, or on the asphalt, don't be shy. They'll love showing you what country plays the game the best.

Let's go play a **pickup game** with the guys from that bar.
*Vamos **bater uma pelada** com os garotos do bar. | ...um baba ...*

Can I join your pickup game?
Posso bater uma pelada com vocês?

Can I **play**?
*Posso **jogar**?*

Nice **cleats**!
*Suas **chuteiras** são legais!*

I'm not that good...
Sou um pouco perna de pau...
Literally, "wooden legged."

What **team** should I be on?
*Em que **time** vou jogar?*

What are the **rules**?
*Quais são as **regras**?*

How many are gonna play?
Quantos na linha?

Hey! I'm **open**, kick it here!
*Aqui! Tô **sózinho**, passa pra mim!*

Nice goal!
Golaço!

sidelines
linhas laterais

out-of-bounds
fora

corner
escanteio

box
grande área

goal area / six-yard box
pequena área

offsides
impedimento

overtime / extra time
prorrogação

stoppage time
acréscimos

running the clock
cera

★★★ At the Stadium
No Estádio

What's your favorite ... ?
Qual é seu/sua... favorito/a ? | Qual é seu...?

team
time

franchise
clube

national team
seleção

Who is the **star** on your team?
*Quem é o **craque** do seu time?*

What time's the **game**?
*Que horas é o **jogo**?*

Who are you rooting for?
Para quem você torce?

I'm **rooting** for/against...
*Tô **torcendo** para/contra...*

> Spain.
> *Espanha.*
>
> Tahiti.
> *Tahiti.*
>
> Brazil, duh!
> *Brasil, claro!*

How much does a **jersey** cost?
*Quanto custa uma **camisa**?*

Where can I buy a **souvenir** from the game?
*Onde compro uma **lembrança** do jogo?*

Where is the **bathroom**?
*Onde é o **banheiro**?*

I need to **take a piss**.
*Preciso **mijar**.*

You better wait, the **line** is out the door.
*Melhor esperar. A **fila** tá lá fora.*

Can you bring me a beer at **halftime**?
*Você pode me trazer uma cerveja no **intervalo**?*
Don't think you'll be saying this at the stadium, unless you want non-alcoholic beer.
That's right, in Brazilian stadiums there is a policy for no alcoholic beverages or
glass bottles.

Where can I buy a **beer**?
*Onde posso comprar uma **cerveja**?*

Cheers
Elogios.

Let's go...
Bora...

> fuck shit up!
> *bota pra fuder!*

> mark your players!
> *marca!*

Thief
Ladrão
Fans yell this to alert their player that someone is going to steal the ball from them from behind.

You may hear some people singing some of the following cheers:

The champion is back!
O campeão voltou!

Hello, "insert rival team here," you can wait, your time is gonna come.
Alô "———" pode esperar, a sua hora vai chegar.
You will hear this a lot in the stadiums in Brazil. Any time a team is going to play against the Brazilian team the fans yell this, "warning" them that their time to be massacred is about to come.

Oh! Jump around and let the cauldron boil!
Uh! Pula aê deixa o caldeirão ferver!

"Fred" will get you!
"Fred" vai te pegar!
The Brazilian player Fred has a song dedicated to him after the horror movie character, Freddy Krueger.

When your team isn't playing so hot
Quando seu time tá jogando mal

Aww, come on!
Haaa, qualé?

That wasn't a foul!
Você inventou essa falta!
Literally, "You made up this foul."

My forward is a corpse.
Meu atacante é uma carniça.

Bad fucking pass!
Bola filha da puta!

Number 10 is a disgrace to my team.
Esse número 10 é uma desgraça.

That foul wasn't for a card?! This fucking ref is making bad calls!
Essa falta não foi pra cartão?! Esse juiz desgraçado tá roubando!

That's an ugly-ass game.
Jogo feio miserável.

This goalie has butter fingers.
Esse goleiro tem mãos de alface.
Literally, "lettuce hands."

What a beast!
Que jogador brucutu!

Gloating
Regozijar

Some things to get started *batendo boca* (shit-talking).

My team's gonna...
Meu time vai...

> dominate.
> *dar uma lavada.*

> score a ton of goals.
> *dar uma goleada.*

> humiliate the other team.
> *dar um chocolate.*
> Kind of like the sweet taste of victory.

> fuck some shit up!
> *botar pra fuder!*

That guy's a **playmaker**.
Esse moleque é **craque**.

This team's fans suffer.
Torcedor desse time sofre.

Goal's wide open — **shoot it!**
Chuta *que o gol tá aberto!*

This team plays well together.
Esse time joga por música.
Literally, "This team plays by music" (kind of like a symphony).

Mexico's team **is crap!**
O time do México **é a treva!**

Swearing
Xingar

Swear words have been around since the grunt of the Neanderthals, so in Brazil it's no different—there's a ton of ways to express your frustration.

Darn!
Caramba!

Shoot!
Miséria!

Shucks!
Diabo!

Cunt!
Buceta!

Dammit!
Porra!

The word *porra* can be anything you want it to be. It can be an exclamation like "dammit," "shit," or "fuck." Or, in attempt to be as confusing as possible, the word can be used as an emphasis, an adverb, a noun, or even a comma.

What the **fuck** kind of a play was that?
*Que **porra** de passe foi aquele?*

What the **hell** is this?
*Que **porra** é essa?*

Your team is **fucking** ugly.
*Seu time é feio como a **porra**.*

The stadium is **hella** far.
*O estadio é longe pra **porra**.*

I don't like this shit.
*Não gosto dessa **porra**.*

Disgrace!
Desgraça!
Believe us, this is a lot stronger in Portuguese.

Shit!
Merda!

Fuck!
Caralho!

Insults
Insultos

Soccer matches get pretty heated. Make sure you're taking your frustrations out on the right people.

Hey ref, take it up the ass!
Ei juiz, vai tomar no cú!

The ref is a...
O juiz é um/uma...

> thief.
> *ladrão.*
>
> son of a bitch.
> *filho da puta.*
>
> cuckold.
> *corno.*
> This is actually one of the worst insults in Brazil, so don't use it lightly.

Number 9 is a...
O número 9 é um/uma...

> liar.
> *enganador.*
>
> bastard.
> *safado/a.*

prick.
pica tonta.
Literally, "dizzy dick."

ho-bag.
ordinário/a.

heifer.
vaca.

bitch.
puta.

dick.
otário.

dumbass.
mané.

idiot.
idiota.

doofus.
comédia.

fuck-up.
vacilão. | cuzão.

Sit down!
Senta!

If people aren't playing by the rules, put 'em in their place, *porra*!

Can you please sit down?
Pode sentar, por favor?

I can't see the game!
Paguei inteira!
Literally, "I payed full price," implying that you want to see the *whole* game.

Sit the fuck down!
Senta, porra!

You talkin' to me?
Tá falando comigo?

If you do find yourself in a confrontation, we aren't advising you to act out, but if you must, remember, it's all in the tone. Some of these phrases aren't really fighting words unless you say them with an ugly glare to go along with it.

What?
Qualé?

Wassup?
Qual foi?

Is there a **problem**?
*Algum **problema**?*

What do you want?
Qual é mesmo?

What are you looking at, fuck-up?
O que você tá olhando, vacilão?

What the fuck are you looking at?
Que porra você tá me olhando?

Do you like dick or something? Why are you looking at me?
Tô com cara de pica? Tá me olhando por que?

Do you not see me, motherfucker?
Não tá me vendo filho da puta?

Is your eye in your asshole?
Tá com o olho no cú?

Get outta my face!
Sai da minha frente!

Get to steppin'.
Vaza mané.

Beat it, dick.
Mete o pé, otário.

I don't want to see your ugly mug again.
Não quero te ver nem pintado de ouro.
Literally, "I don't want to see you even if you are painted with gold."

Go to hell!
Vai pro inferno! | Vai pra porra!

Take your hands off me!
Tira sua mão de mim!

Get lost, you creep.
Vai ver se eu tô na esquina.
Literally, "Go see if I'm around the corner."

Screw you!
Vai se danar!

Go back to the bitch that made you!
Vai pra puta que pariu!

Up yours!
Vai tomar no cú!

Piss off!
Vai se ferrar!

Fuck off!
Vai se lenhar!

Go fuck yourself!
Vai se fuder!

Shut up!
Cala a boca!

Shut your piehole!
***Fecha** essa boca! | o bico!*

I don't wanna talk about it!
Nem vem que não tem!

Quit sayin' that!
Vira essa boca pra lá!

You talk a lot a **bullshit**.
*Você só fala **merda**.*

Fightin' words
Palavras de briga

We aren't advising you to start hurling insults or threatening any other spectators. If you must, though, you might get some local appreciation if you use Portuguese.

Say that one more time if you have the guts.
Repita isso se você for homem.

I'll fuck your team up.
Eu vou fuder o seu time.

Let's **fight** man to man.
*Vamos **brigar** mano a mano.*

Shit's about to go down!
O coro vai comer!

You're gonna lose, motherfucker!
Vai acabar dançando, filho da puta!

Better stop **pushing** me, I don't wanna have to get rough with you.
*Melhor parar de me **empurrar**, não quero ter que bater em você.*

I'm gonna kick your ass.
Eu vou surrar você.

I'm gonna **break** your face in half.
*Eu vou **partir** a sua cara no meio.*

They **fucked shit up** last night.
*Eles **quebraram o pau** ontem à noite.*

If you don't get outta that chair my finger's going in your asshole.
Levanta dessa cadeira, senão vou dar uma dedada no seu cú.

Chill out
Calma

Let it go.
Deixa disso.

Forget about it.
Deixa isso pra lá.

It's not worth it.
Não vale a pena.

Calm down, man.
***Calma**, rapaz.*

Chill brah, there's nothing we can do about it.
***Fica na sua** broder, estamos de mãos atadas.*

Get a hold of yourself!
Segura tua onda!

I made a mistake.
Dei um fora.

Take it easy!
Pega leve! | Esfria a cabeça!

Take it down a notch.
Abaixa sua crista.
Literally, "Let down your rooster comb."

Forget it, my brother.
Esquece isso, mermão.

Stay outta this.
Fica fora disso.

Take it outside.
Vai brigar lá fora.

I don't want to **fight** you.
*Não quero **brigar** com você.*

Let's have a beer and **forget** about this.
*Vamos tomar uma cerveja e **esquecer** isso.*

CHAPTER 4

THE BEAUTIFUL GAME
Futebol Arte

Now that you're fully prepped to talk the talk during matches, it's time to brush up on your actual knowledge of the game, the teams, and their players. We'll brief you on some basic info on the stadiums and a mini history lesson on each city's soccer scene...because really, that's the main thing that matters to Brazilians: their national soccer club.

★★★ Technical Talk
Fala Técnica

What team are you **rooting** for?
*Para que time você **torce**?*

Everyone knows who is **favored** to win.
*Todo mundo sabe quem é o **favorito**.*

Fuck Spain. All they do is **pass** the ball back and forth!
*Esquece a Espanha. Eles só **passam** a bola de um lado pra outro.*

I really like Spain's **style of** passing.
*Gosto muito do **toque de bola** da Espanha.*

There isn't a better **defense** than Italy's.
*Não tem **defesa** melhor que a da seleção italiana.*

It's going to be a steep **competition**.
*A **competição** vai ser muito grande.*

They are so...
Eles são tão...

> quick.
> *rápidos.*

> agile.
> *ágeis.*

> good at attacking.
> *bons no ataque.*

> good at counter-attacking.
> *bons de contra-ataque.*

They have a solid **offense/defense**.
*Eles são bons na parte **ofensiva/defensiva**.*

Friendly
Amistoso

Qualifiers
Eliminatórias

Qualified
Classificado

Bracket
Grupo

Group play
Fase de grupos

Seed
Cabeça de chave

First round
Primeira fase

Round of 16
Oitavas de finais

Quarter finals
Quartas de finais

Semifinals
Semi finais

Final
Final

Eliminated
Eliminado

Draw
Empate

Win
Vitória

Loss
Derrota

Unexpected loss
Cavalo paraguaio
Literally, "Paraguayan horse." In Brazil, *paraguaio* is slang for "bad quality" because the cheap stuff sold on the black market is usually from Paraguay. In soccer context, it describes a team that does very well in the beginning of the tournament but blows it in the end (because of its poor quality).

Unfavored win
Zebra
When an underdog wins a game against a stronger team. The expression came
from an illegal lottery-type game in Brazil where you place bets, associating
numbers with animals. Since the zebra is NOT one of the animals, it's
impossible for the "zebra" to win.

★★★ The Local Soccer Scene
Futebol Local

Each host city has a lot of passion not only for Brazil but more importantly
their regional teams, which fall into four different leagues or levels (called
séries): A, B, C, and D, depending on their ranking (with Série A being the
most competitive bracket). If you want to show you know a little about where
you are, read up on where the local soccer pride lies. At least you know it will
be a sure way of striking up a lively conversation.

Manaus, Amazonas

Teams: Nacional, Rio Negro

Manaus is not well-known for *futebol* so there are no big-name Série A teams.
Nacional and Rio Negro are the two regional clubs, both founded in 1913
around the time of the rubber boom that put Manaus on the map. Today, you
won't hear about these teams outside the state of Amazonas.

Fortaleza, Ceará

Teams: Ceará, Fortaleza

The city of Fortaleza is in the state of Ceará, host two of the major
nordeste (northeast) region teams: Ceará and Fortaleza. Ceará's biggest
accomplishments were advancing to the semis of Copa do Brasil in 2005
and 2011. Even though both teams are not in the top *séries* of the national
tournament, they still bring out considerable crowds to the arenas, giving

both teams perennial spots on the list of clubs that attract the largest numbers of fans to the stadiums.

Natal, Rio Grande do Norte
Teams: ABC, América de Natal

With its faultless tropical climate that averages 300 sunny days per year, it's no surprise that Natal is the perfect setting for some amazing football. ABC is the oldest soccer club in Rio Grande do Norte. It was named in honor of the ABC Powers, Argentina, Brazil, and Chile, who united in 1915 to resist U.S. influence in the region. The América, or América de Natal, is the only team from Natal that has won a regional tournament (Copa do Nordeste, 1998).

Recife, Pernambuco
Teams: Sport, Náutico, Santa Cruz

Recife's residents are die-hard soccer fans — perhaps the most passionate in the country. Sport is the most successful of the three teams (they've already won the Campeonato Brasileiro once); their biggest rival is Náutico. Santa Cruz (who just made it back to Série B) has been playing the worst soccer in their history, but even so, in 2011 they had the best average of the season between all *séries* of the Brazilian Championship.

Salvador, Bahia
Teams: Bahia, Vitória

In Salvador it's simple: You are either Bahia or you are Vitória (also known as VICE). One of the oldest teams in the country, Vitória has won a number of state championships since the 1990s, but they've never won the nationals. With two national championships under its belt, Bahia has the majority of fans in the state. The team is particularly proud and honored to have been the first team to win the nationals against the unbeatable Santos during the reign of Pelé. Bahia has experienced a few ups and downs over the years, but has returned to playing in the first tier of soccer, where it hopefully will remain forever. *Bora Bahia Minha Porra* ("Let's Go Bahia, Dammit")!

Brazilian Football League System
Sistema de Ligas de Futebol do Brasil

It's no surprise that there's a wildly popular national soccer league in Brazil. Here's how it works. The soccer teams fall into four levels, or *séries*: A, B, C, and D, with A as the top division. Teams move between the levels based on how they did the previous season, but in general, the more financially comfortable clubs are consistently in Série A while the rest compete to win spots in the top-tier *séries*. Séries A, B, and C each have 20 teams, while the bottom level D has 40. At the end of the year, the worst top-four teams of Séries A, B, and C are relegated to a lower level, and the top-four clubs in Séries B, C, and D move up one division. The Copa do Brasil is held every year, and the competitors are based on the previous year's highest-ranking teams or their position at the end of the state championships.

Teams also participate in their state league system (set up similarly to the national pyramid system), with each state holding its own annual championship. While there are parallels to the national system, many details are different, like the number of teams in each level or specific rules.

Bottom line: If you're looking to watch a soccer game, there are lots of options out there for you.

Mato Grosso, Cuiabá

Teams: Mixto Cuiabá, Dom Bosco, Operário

Although people in the *Cidade Verde* (Green City) are as passionate about soccer as the rest of their countrymen, the regional teams are neither well-known nor highly ranked. Mixto Esporte Clube is the most important of the teams. The Mixto's main city rivals are Cuiabá, Dom Bosco, and Operário, which is in the neighboring city of Várzea.

Brasília, Brasília DF

Teams: Gama, Brasiliense

The country's newest big city, Brasília, is also new to the soccer leagues. This is reflected in the lowly rank of Brasília's two main teams: Brasiliense, established in 2000 and currently in Série C, and Gama (or Verdão, meaning "big green"), who is currently not even qualified for Série D. In 2002, Brasiliense were actually finalists in the Copa do Brasil, losing to the Corinthians in the finals, quite a feat for such a young team.

Belo Horizonte, Minas Gerais

Teams: Atlético Mineiro (Galo), Cruzeiro (Raposa), América Mineiro (Coelho)

The oldest club in Belo Horizonte, Atlético Mineiro (or Galo, meaning "rooster") is known as a "people's team." With a history full of accomplishments, it's greatest glory came in 2013 when Ronaldinho (yes, the one from Barcelona) lead Atlético in winning the prestigious Libertadores da América. Cruzeiro (or Raposa, meaning "fox") is one of the most successful soccer clubs in Brazil and the only team to have won three important titles in the same year (2003). They are also the current Série A champs. The América Mineiro (or Coelho, meaning "rabbit") won the Série B title in 2004; they now partner with the Tahitian Football Federation to develop young players.

Rio de Janeiro, Rio de Janeiro

Teams: Flamengo, Botafogo, Fluminense, Vasco

RJ *is* Brazilian soccer; everywhere you look, there it is. It's no wonder that superstar players like Jairzinho, Zico, Ronaldo, and Romário all played in Rio. Competition for talent is fierce among the clubs, which constantly vie for attention and prestige. The most popular of the popular is Flamengo. With five national championships and a couple of international titles, Flamengo was home to Zico, a Brazilian soccer "god." It's also said to have the largest number of fans on the planet, around 50 million.

Second in popularity is Vasco de Gama, or Vasco. The team was named after Portuguese explorer Vasco de Gama, who was the first European to travel from Europe to India.

Vasco is a four-time Série A champion; the current team president is Vasco's retired striker Roberto Dinamite, the club's all-time top scorer.

Founded in 1902, Fluminense was one of the first clubs to roster black players, who used to powder their faces with rice flour to appear white during matches (a practice born out of the racist *carioca* society that did not approve of desegregated teams). In the 1990s, Fluminense went down to Série C (lowest level at the time) but returned to Série A with some dramatic ups and downs (like the year they were almost demoted to Série B then rallied the following year to win the National Championship).

And then there's Botafogo, the Rio team with the least number of national titles (just one, and that was due to an irregular goal). The team hasn't had much glory in the past decade, but since the Netherland's Seedorf joined the squad in 2012, Botafogo's visibility has heightened. Zagallo, the only person to win four soccer World Cups (1958, 1964, 1970, 2004) played for Botafogo.

São Paulo, São Paulo

Teams: Corinthians, São Paulo, Palmeiras, Santos

With some of the best players in the country and solid financial backing, the state of São Paulo has a number of very good teams, with the capital city boasting four dominating ones: Corinthians, São Paulo, Palmeiras, and Santos.

Corinthians has the second-largest number of fans in the country and coincidentally, according to recent surveys, is also the most hated. The New York Yankees of Brazilian football, the team has won five national titles (and a few international ones) and is Brazil's richest soccer club ($358 million). Their fans, mostly from the lower class, are called *Fiel*, or "Faithful," because they follow the team everywhere it goes — even to Japan for the 2012 FIFA Club World Cup, a mighty distance but well worth the trip for the devoted. Soccer rivals often equate a *Fiel* to a criminal because many São Paulo prison inmates are Corinthians fans who aren't bothered by this anecdotal characterization.

São Paulo is the winningest team and also the youngest; they've won six national championships, three Libertadores, and various international titles. Another extremely wealthy team, São Paulo has the biggest private stadium in the country and fans that draw from the city's middle class. Their goalie, Rogério Ceni, is in the *Guinness Book of World Records* for the goalkeeper who has scored the most goals than any other goalie in the history of soccer (111 and counting).

Originally named Palestra Itália, the club name was changed to Palmeiras during World War II when Italy-related names and customs were prohibited in Brazil to disassociate the country from Mussolini's oppressive dictatorship (this happened with a lot of clubs during this period, including Cruzeiro in Belo Horizonte). However, the unconditional love and support of the city's Italian immigrants (along with a large portion of *paulistas* and the rest of the country) maintained and continues to maintain Palmeiras as one of the more popular teams in the country, attracting internationally known players such as Roberto Carlos and Rivaldo. The team has won eight national titles and a couple of others, including a Série B.

Santos isn't actually located in the capital proper, but they definitely have a spot among the country's greatest clubs. The Fishes (or *Peixes*), as they are known, are very proud of their soccer schools—the very same ones that helped develop greats like Pelé, Robinho, and recently Neymar. They are, as Brazilians say, *uma fábrica de craques* ("a factory of star players"). They have eight national titles and three Libertadores. During the '60s and '70s, they became a global phenomenon, traveling the world to play exhibition matches. In 1969, Santos even prompted a break in Nigeria's bitter civil war, the bloodiest in Africa's history.

Curitiba, Paraná

Teams: Coritiba, Atlético Paranaense, Paraná Clube

Curitiba is home to three teams: Coritiba, Atlético Paranaense, and Paraná Clube. The state's oldest club, Coritiba was founded in 1909 and is known as (believe it or not), Coxa Branca, or "White Thigh." The club is the best ranked team in the CBF (Confederação Brasileira de Futebol) and the FIFA classification, and jumps between Séries A and B. Lately, Coritiba has been signing better players, leading to stronger squads.

Atlético Paranaense, nicknamed Furacão (Hurricane), was established in 1924. Atlético was the first *Paranaense* club to participate in the Campeonato Brasileiro Série A, winning the title for the first time in 2001. A third team worth noting is Paraná Clube, well-known in the soccer world losing popularity in the Série B.

Porto Alegre, Rio Grande do Sul

Teams: Grêmio, Internacional de Porto Alegre

Grêmio is a rich, very-well-organized team and was superstar Ronaldinho's first club. Even though they were in the Série B a while ago, they are now a strong team that has won one Intercontinental Cup, two Copa Libertadores, two Campeonatos Brasileiros, and four Copas do Brasil. Though they aren't hosting any World Cup games, they just completed construction on a new stadium (probably because their rival Inter is an official host and has remodeled their arena).

Inter is also known as Colorado or Vermelho (the Red) for their color. This club is a three-time Recopa Sulamericana champion, two-time Copa Libertadores champ, and a FIFA Club World Cup winner. They are the state champions 42 times over.

The Gre-Nal rivalry began in 1909 when Gremio swept Inter, 10-0 during a match, soon after Inter was founded. They've been at each other's throats since that day. The soccer in Porto Alegre has a strong youth soccer program, and they've got Alexandre Pato and Ronaldinho (FIFA World Player of the Year 2004–05) to show for it.

★★★ The Stadiums
Os Estádios

Stadiums, like the soccer clubs, all have nicknames. None of the venues go by the official name emblazoned above the main entrance, so don't get confused when you arrive at what your friends call Maracanã and the sign says Estádio Jornalista Mário Filho — it's the same place. For your convenience, we've included the arena nicknames in parenthesis.

Arena Amazônia (Vivaldão)
Manaus, Amazonas
Capacity: around 46,000

Surrounded by hotels and shops, Vivaldão is located close to the airport and downtown Manaus. The stadium is the "greenest" of the 12 World Cup venues, not just because of its setting in the Amazon rainforest, but also for the way it was sustainably built—95 percent of the materials from the old stadium were recycled for the new one.

Estádio Governador Plácido Castelo (Castelão)

Fortaleza, Ceará

Capacity: around 65,000 | Number of World Cup Games: 6

Built in the 1970s, Castelão is one of the largest stadiums in the country. Renovations have given this dated facility an impressively chic and modern look.

Arena das Dunas (Machadão)

Natal, Rio Grande do Norte

Capacity: around 42,000 | Number of World Cup Games: 4

A brand-new stadium, Machadão received praise and awards for its modern design. The official name, Arena das Dunas ("Dune Stadium") is a nod to Natal's main tourist attraction: the rolling sand dunes.

Itaipava Arena Pernambuco

Recife, Pernambuco

Capacity: around 46,000

The Recife stadium isn't actually in Recife; it's about 19 kilometers west of the city. Locals refer to the area surrounding Arena Pernambuco as "Cup City."

Itaipava Arena Fonte Nova (Fonte Nova)

Salvador, Bahia

Capacity: around 50,000

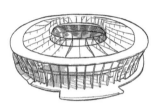

Fonte Nova, or "New Fountain," was built in the early 1950s but closed in 2007 due to a tragic accident when a piece of the structurally unsound bleachers broke, killing seven people. The old stadium was demolished to make way for a modern, state-of-the-art facility up to FIFA standards. The horseshoe-shaped stadium is centrally located with beautiful views of nearby Dique de Tororó lake.

Arena Pantanal (Verdão)

Cuiabá, Mato Grosso

Capacity: around 43,000

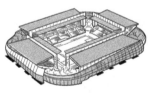

Verdão is smack dab in the wetlands of Brazil, but don't worry, the stadium isn't in the middle of a swamp. While the structure is completely new, the stadium was constructed with much of the materials from its predecessor, Estádio Governador José Fragelli. This sustainable decision has given Arena Pantanal its nickname, Verdão (Big Green).

Estádio Nacional de Brasília Mané Garrincha (Estádio Nacional)

Brasília, Brasília DF
Capacity: around 70,000

Brasília's old Estádio Nacional de Brasília Mané Garrincha (formerly just Estádio Mané Garrincha) was named in honor of the Brazilian soccer hero who was a two-time world champion. The structure was demolished in 2010 to make way for a new stadium, whose name was shortened by FIFA to just Estádio Nacional.

Estádio Governador Magalhães Pinto (Mineirão)

Belo Horizonte, Minas Gerais
Capacity: around 62,000

A stadium was constructed in Belo Horizonte for the first World Cup in 1950, but within two decades, it was determined that a bigger and more modern arena was needed. So in 1965, Estádio Governador Magalhães Pinto, twice the size of the original stadium, was built next to Pampulha lake. Mineirão stadium has been hosting important games like the Championship Finals and Brazilian national team games ever since. Renovations to Mineirão's outdated audio video system were done to meet FIFA standards.

Estádio Jornalista Mário Filho (Maracanã)

Rio de Janeiro, Rio de Janeiro

Capacity: around 77,000

Maracanã, the second most visited tourist spot in Rio, needs no introduction to football fans. The stadium was built for the first FIFA World Cup in 1950 and is where Brazil became one of the few teams to lose a final World Cup game in their own country. Despite that dubious distinction, Maracanã is the most important stadium in Brazil and, all modesty aside, one of the most important on the planet. The arena has played host to national and international matches for years, and has been called "the biggest stadium in the world" stemming from the ridiculous amounts of fans that have shown up for matches, most notably the 1950 World Cup final between Brazil and Uruguay which drew 200,000 people to the arena.

Arena São Paulo (Itaquerão)

São Paulo, São Paulo

Capacity: around 66,000

Privately owned by the Corinthians (the second most popular soccer club in the country), Itaquerão was already in the midst of construction when Brazil was chosen to host the World Cup in 2014, so the plans were adapted to meet FIFA's standards. Keep in mind that the stadium isn't located anywhere near downtown São Paulo, one the biggest cities in the world (it's the seventh most populous).

Estádio Joaquim Américo Guimarães (Arena da Baixada)
Curitiba, Paraná
Capacity: around 42,000

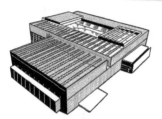

Relatively small compared to the other stadiums, the Arena da Baixada is another private stadium. The structure was renovated in 1999 and at that time received the title of most modern stadium in Latin America.

Estádio José Pinheiro Borda (Beira-Rio)
Porto Alegre, Rio Grande do Sul
Capacity: around 56,000

The Estádio Beira-Rio is one of the biggest private stadiums in the country. Renovated in the 1960s, it once held the record in the *Guinness Book of World Records* for the largest movie screening session, with more than 27,000 people in attendance of the *Absoluto-Inter, Bicampeão da América*, a documentary about...*futebol*.

CHAPTER 5

Party Time
Hora da Festa

Brazil is one of the best party destinations on the planet. Brazilians know how to do it big, whether it's at a club, in a bar, at the beach, or just on the side of the road with giant speakers booming from the trunk of a car.

★★★ Watching the Game
Assistindo o Jogo

Just head to the corner bar, the *lanchonete* (café), or the city's designated *fan fest* (fan area). Believe us, the party will be just as happening, if not more so, outside than inside the stadium. Remember this: When Brazil plays, the entire country watches. Which means the entire country shuts down since no one wants to miss the game. You won't be able to pop over to the grocery store at half time to grab some more beers—the streets will be deserted other than the areas that are open for screening the game.

Where are you watching the **game**?
*Vai assistir o **jogo** aonde?*

Where is a good place to watch the game around here?
Onde tem um lugar bom pra assistir o jogo perto daqui?

Where is a cool **bar** to watch the game?
Onde tem um bar legal pra assistir o jogo?

I'm going to a cool **little bar**.
*Vou pra um **barzinho** bem legal.*

We're heading to the **neighborhood bar**. You wanna come?
*A gente vai no **bar da esquina**. Tá a fim?*

Don't assume you'll be in an air-conditioned sports bar. Most bars are tiny holes-in-the-wall with plastic tables and chairs; the TV is located outside for patrons to watch the game from the street.

Pre-gaming
Pré-festa

Tailgaiting is done a little differently here – you don't have to haul in massive amounts of gear and food to the stadium. Everything you need – beer, barbecue, snacks – is already right there in the arena parking lot (or at least located very near). Vendors do the set-up and cater to all your pre-gaming needs. Because of FIFA regulations, the vendors are not going to be at the parking lots as they normally are, but if you go a bit further you'll be sure to find them and you better get your fixings before the game because once inside the stadium, everything will be at least five times more expensive. When Brazil is playing, *brasileiros* who aren't going to the stadium will gather at a house before the game for *cerveja* (beer) and *churrasco* (barbecue). But once the clock starts running, the focus is all on *futebol*. If you're invited to one of these *festinhas*, that's cool – you've made a friend. Don't worry about bringing anything to put on the grill – just contribute a few bucks to the host.

There's an awesome restaurant that's **showing** the game.
*Tem um restaurante bem legal **passando** o jogo.*

Let's have a **barbecue** and watch the game.
*Vamos fazer um **churrasco** e assistir o jogo.*

How much is a **tall can**?
*Quanto é o **latão**?*
Usually there's some kind of deal if you get more than one.

Can I have two **skewers**, please?
*Dois **churrascos** por favor.*

I can't see anything, can we move **closer**?
*Não consigo ver nada, vamos **mais pra frente**?*

★★★ Post-Game Partying
Festejando Depois do Jogo

The night isn't over when the clock runs out—it has only just begun.

Let's...
Vamos...

> go out.
> *sair.*

> stop by that **party**.
> *dar uma passada naquele **festa**.*

> tell (invite) everyone.
> *chamar geral.*

> go clubbing.
> *pra balada.*

> grab a drink at the **bar**.
> *tomar uma no **bar**. | **boteco**. | **barzinho**.*

go to the **club**.
pra ***boate***.

go to the **strip clubs**.
*pro **clube de striper***.

go back to the **hotel**.
*voltar pro **hotel***.

Forget the game, I wanna **dance**.
*Esquece o jogo, quero **dançar***.

Let's find a bar that has **live music**.
*Vamos para um bar que tenha **música ao vivo***.

We're all going to an **underground dance club**, wanna join?
*A gente vai pra um **baile funk**, tá a fim?*
Baile funk is an underground club often found in the *favelas* in Rio de Janeiro that play *funk carioca* (page 98) into the early morning.

Are you down?
Você topa?

> I'm down.
> *Topo. | Tô nessa. | Tô dentro.*

> **I'm out.** I'm so tired from that game.
> ***Tô fora.** Tô cansado pra caramba por causa do jogo.*

Wanna go?
Você quer ir?

> Yeah!
> *Quero!*
> Questions are rarely answered with *sim* or *não*. Use the present tense of the verb instead.

> Next time. I'm feeling **lazy** today.
> *Fica pra próxima. Tô com **preguiça** hoje.*

> Maybe.
> *Pode ser.*

What's **happening** tonight?
*O que **tá rolando** hoje à noite?*

Don't worry, I'll **show up**.
*Fica tranquilo que eu vou **aparecer**.*

I'll make an appearance.
Vou dar uma chegada.

LGBT Scene
Cenário GLS

Brazil is a free country when it comes to expressing yourself. It welcomes the LGBT community with *braços abertos* (open arms). The end of June marks Gay Pride, which is as big a celebration in Rio de Janeiro and São Paulo as it is in San Francisco's Castro District. In Rio, most of the gay nightlife is centered in the Leblon neighborhood just west of Ipanema and Copacabana. In São Paulo the gay scene is mainly located in the district of Consolação on Rua Frei Caneca. While the gay scene is a little more underground in other cities, just ask around. There are plenty of gay venues to peruse no matter what major city you find yourself in.

Do you know of any **gay clubs** around here?
*Tem alguma **boate gay** por aqui?*

Where is the **LGBT scene** in this city?
*Onde tá o **cenário GLS** (Gays, Lésbicas, e simpatizantes) nessa cidade?*

There's some nice **eye candy** over in that corner.
*Tem uns **bofes** do lado de lá.*
Bofe is slang for "liver" as well. If you are talking eye candy in a straighter sense, use *colírio*.

Look at Márcio, he's **cruising** tonight!
*Olha o Márcio, tá **caçando** essa noite!*
Generally the word *caçar* (to hunt), is used for men who don't identify as gay but are looking for some brotherly affection at the moment.

After so much partying I need a **sauna**.
*Depois de tanta festa, preciso duma **sauna**.*

That girl in the **VIP** section is super hot.
*Aquela mina no **camarote** é muito gostosa.*

I'm...
Sou...

gay.
gay. | viado. | biba.
Viado is derogatory but friendly when it's used by another gay man.

lesbian.
lésbica.

queer.
bicha.

transgender.
transgênero.

a transvestite.
um travesti.

Cross-dressers are fairly common in Brazil. In fact, during Carnaval there are entire *blocos* (parade groups) that feature men who exclusively dress as women. But don't be misled by the feminine clothing – most of these men are not gay or even bisexual.

★★★ Booze
Birita

Just like in Europe, beer is by far the beverage of choice, followed by *caipirinhas*, mixed drinks made with *cachaça* (a liquor similar to rum), sugar, and lime.

Can I buy you a drink?
Posso te pagar uma bebida?

Do you want anything to drink?
Quer beber alguma coisa?

I want...
Eu quero...

> a drink.
> *uma bebida.* | *um goró.*

> a *cachaça*.
> *uma cachaça.*
> Brazil's version of rum, this spirit is made from fermented sugarcane
> juice. It's most commonly drunk in a fruity concoction, but you can also
> find the good stuff, spiced with different herbs, and drink it straight.
> This drink is everywhere (it's also known as *pinga* and *aguardente*).

> a caipirinha.
> *uma caipirinha.*
> Mmmm...who doesn't love the light cocktail made from *cachaça*, sugar,
> crushed limes, and ice.

> a caipiroska.
> *uma caipiroska.*
> Cocktail made of vodka, sugar, fruit of choice (strawberries, limes,
> kiwi...), and ice.

> a glass of wine.
> *um copo de vinho.*
> You can get red (*tinto*) or white (*branco*), but try to go for the
> Argentinean or Chilean brands because the Brazilian wine is as sweet as
> Manischewitz.

> a chaser.
> *uma bebida fraca.*

> a shot.
> *uma dose.*

> brandy.
> *conhaque.*

rum.
rum.

whiskey.
uísque.

vodka.
vodka.

tequila.
tequila.

liquor.
licor.

champagne.
champanhe.

cider.
sidra.

beer.
cerveja.

Beer
Cerveja

What's better than an ice cold beer on a hot tropical day? It's the drink of choice from the bars to the beach. No matter what time of day, it's always time for beer. Sadly, Brazil is not known for its artisan ales or dark lagers. There's pretty much just one type — light and smooth. Occasionally you can find *Moçambique* which is a dark, sweet beer, but the majority of bottles being poured are equivalent to a PBR or a Corona, something that goes down quick in the heat of the day. *Cerveja* is ordered by the bottle and drunk from *copinhos* (mini glasses), except at the beach or in the street, where you can buy it by the can. Draft beer is not served in pints, but don't freak out, the *chopp* (draft beer) will keep coming and coming and coming until you decide you're done. So, down the hatch!

Count your bottles!
Conte as suas garrafas!

Make sure to keep track of the number of bottles you and your buddies have consumed. Depending on the facility, they will either leave the bottles on or by your table to count up when you're ready to pay the bill or you'll have a *comanda*, a slip of paper that keeps a tally of what you've ordered. If it's a pile of empty bottles or stacks of coasters (used when ordering from the tap), then keep an eye on it. Sometimes a server might try to slip an extra bottle or two in there to get you to pay for more than you asked for. This is especially prevalent at the beach or with a large party of tourists who look like they aren't paying attention! And if they use *comandas*, don't lose it – the cost of a lost slip is normally written on the bottom of the *comanda*, and can be a lot more expensive than a few beers.

Let's have...
Vamos tomar...

> a bottle of beer.
> *uma garrafa de cerveja.*
>
> a brew.
> *uma cerva. | brisa.*
>
> an ale.
> *um gel.*
>
> a draft.
> *um chopp.*
>
> a cold one.
> *uma gelada.*
>
> a tall one.
> *um latão.*
> This refers to a tall can.
>
> a pale ale.
> *uma lora.*
> Short for *loira*, which means "blond."

Can I get an **ice-cold beer?**
*Me traz uma cerveja **bem gelada**?*

Let's grab a ridiculously cold brew.
Vamos pegar uma cerva estupidamente gelada.

Boozing
Embebedando-se

We told you the rounds just keep coming. If you're lucky though, it has loosened up your tongue.

Let's get **a drink.**
*Vamos tomar **uma birita**. | **uma**. | **um copo**.*

Tonight I don't wanna worry about anything, **I'm going on a binge.**
*Hoje não quero saber de nada, vou **encher a cara**.*

Cheers!
Saúde! | Tintin!

One more!
Mais uma!

Next **round's** on me.
*A próxima **rodada** é minha.*

I'm...
Tô...

> tipsy.
> *de pileque.*
>
> drunk.
> *bêbado/a.*
>
> wasted.
> *travado/a.*

What kind of drunk are you?
Que tipo de bêbado você é?

Sleepy drunk
O bebo-bosta

Touchy-feely drunk
O sensível

Funny drunk
O palhaço

Quiet drunk
O altista

Friendly drunk
O amistoso

Happy drunk
O alegre

Angry drunk
O valentão

The drunk who thinks he's the shit
O fodão

Neanderthal drunk
O bêbado Neanderthal

The drunk that can't speak in complete sentences and grunts
a lot.

Mr. "It's time to bring up old shit that you've done"
O lavador de roupa suja

Literally, "the dirty clothes washer." So much for forgive and forget.
This drunk just can't seem to give it a rest. Like the saying goes: *in
vino veritas*.

Mrs. "I'm so fat, aren't I?"
Senhorita "oh, eu sou tão gorda"

When she's drunk, her insecurities are magnified.

smashed.
bebum.

loaded.
embriagado/a.

woozy.
tonto/a.

Let's **get Julia drunk**! She needs to chill out.
*Vamos **embebedar a Julia**. Ela precisa relaxar.*

Check out Gonçalo. Every time he drinks, he gets hammered and ends up **making a fool of himself.**
*Olha o Gonçalo, toda vez que ele bebe, acaba perdendo a linha e **pagando mico**.*
Pagando mico literally translates as "paying a little monkey."

That dude is on a **bender**!
*Esse cara está numa **bebedeira**!*

★★★ Drugs
Drogas

To be clear—drugs are illegal in Brazil. That's not to say they're hard to find (although it may be hard to find anything of quality). Be aware of your surroundings before you choose to light up. With so many foreigners in town, the police will be on the prowl.

Marijuana
Maconha

Do you wanna smoke some...?
Quer fumar...?

weed
bagulho

herb
erva

a joint
um fininho

a doobie
uma marola

a doob
um baseado

Let's...
Vamos...

smoke.
fumar.

light up.
dar dois.
Literally, "to give a deuce."

blaze.
dar um tapa na pantera.
Literally, "to slap a panther."

burn one.
chapar coco.
Literally, "to grill coconut."

toke a doobie.
puxar um beck.
Beck is slang for a longneck of beer...it's also a term for a defender on the soccer field.

Can I light up here?
Posso fumar aqui?

Let's get **high**.
*Vamos **fazer a cabeça**.*

Do you want to buy some **herb**?
*Você quer comprar um pouco de **erva**?*

Do you know where can I **score an ounce**?
*Você sabe onde posso **arrumar um peso**?*

Ask Carlos, he's a **stoner**.
*Pergunta pro Carlos, ele é **chincheiro**. | **maconheiro**.*

You gotta go to a **drug corner**.
*Você tem que ir **na boca**.*

Cocaine
Cocaína

I wanna...
Eu quero...

> sniff some **blow**.
> *cheirar uma **brizola**. | **rapa**. | **poeira**. | **farinha**.*

> powder my nose.
> *meter a napa no pó.*

Forget it, he's too **amped up**.
*Deixa pra lá, ele **tá ligadão**.*

I've never smoked **crack**.
*Nunca fumei **crack**. | **pedra**.*

Careful of the **crackheads** asking for powdered milk!
*Cuidado com os **pedreiros** pedindo por leite em pó! | **sacizeiros***

★★★ Cultural Celebrations and Music
Celebrações Culturais e Música

Brazil has a lot more going on than just *futebol* and alcohol. The country finds a reason to celebrate almost every day of the year. There are holidays for saints, *orixás* (Afro-Brazilian gods), and historic figures, along with Labor Day, Women's Day, and a slew of other hallowed occasions. We're not even going to go into details on all the days honoring saints, because that would take forever. So we've highlighted Carnaval and Festas Juninas (June Festival—because you are going in June). Most importantly though, we'll discuss what is behind every celebration or any Brazilian party in general—*a música*.

Carnival
Carnaval

World renowned for its elaborate costumes, hot dancing, and amazing show, Carnaval is the highlight of the year in Brazil. It's really what the year revolves around and it's the biggest, baddest party in the world. Salvador's Carnaval doesn't traditionally feature the endless parade of fantastic floats and samba schools like in the iconic Rio Carnaval, but you will experience the largest street party Brazil has to offer with awesome music, hoards of partiers, and uninhibited, smoking-hot fun.

In Salvador, *axé* music (page 97) runs the party. It's four days of nonstop revelry (although the parties generally go on for six days) in the streets with music blaring Salvador's favorite singers and bands atop grand floats. People pay to walk and dance along with the float, and everyone wears a T-shirt representing what *bloco* (group) they are in. They're not playing around. Salvador's Carnaval is in the *Guiness Book of World Records* as the biggest street party in the world—probably because every year there's an average of 2 million people celebrating Carnaval here.

Did you see Carlinhos Brown's **float** this year? It was awesome!
*Você viu o **trio elétrico** do Carlinhos Brown esse ano? Foi massa!*
Trio elétrico is an electric float that the singers and bands ride on through the streets.

Where do I buy a T-shirt for Daniela Mercury's **group**?
*Onde compro a camiseta do **bloco** da Daniela Mercury?*
The *bloco* includes the *trio elétrico* and the group of people surrounding it. It's blocked off from the rest of the people by a big rope.

Let's jump around!
Vamos pular!
Since the streets are filled with people there's no room to actually dance. *Axé* music has a beat you can just jump around to and that is exactly what you do alongside the thousands of others: *pula* to the beat.

I'm broke. This year I'm just going to be in the **crowd**.
*Tô duro. Esse ano vou ficar na **pipoca**.*
Pipoca (literally, "popcorn") are the people on the other side of the rope (i.e., those not part of a *bloco*). While they can't walk next to a float, they can jump around to any and all of the groups (like popcorn). Be careful here because a lot of thefts and fights occur.

I'm tired of getting my ass grabbed. Let's go to a **club** tomorrow night.
*Tô cansado/a de ter minha bunda apertada, vamos pra um **camorote** amanhã.*
People who don't want to be squeezed in with a million people on the street can watch from above in clubs built exclusively for Carnaval (then taken down at the end of the week). We're not saying they aren't crowded, too, but it's a little less invasive.

June Festival
Festas Juninas

If you're hitting up Salvador, Recife, Natal, or even Fortaleza, consider taking a trip to a city in the *interior* (countryside) for a few days to experience the most authentic of Festas Juninas colloquially called Festas de São João, their main holiday. Not only is the northeast the best place for these festivities, it's where it is most heavily celebrated in the country. Festas Juninas are a celebration of three catholic saints—Anthony (Antônio), John (João), and Peter (Pedro). The festivities vary from place to place and in some are just celebrated on the saints' respective days, but in cities like Caruaru and Campina Grande, it's a month of country-style mayhem. Because of its countryside tradition, people dress up as farmers—men clad with straw hats and flannel shirts and women donning pigtails, painted freckles, and gap teeth. Get down square dance-style to *forró* music, which will be playing all month long (other types of music are actually prohibited in some cities!). The food is another perk to Festa de São João, with loads of corn-based treats and plenty of uniquely flavored liqueurs.

Let's hit up that ***arraial***.
*Vamos pro **arraial**.*
An *arraial* is a large tent, usually made from natural materials. It's the main venue of these square-dancing shindigs.

Let's see the **bonfire**.
*Vamos ver a **fogueira**.*
There's usually a bonfire at night where you can roast corn on the cob.

I can't sleep with all those **fireworks**!
*Não consigo dormir com todos esses **fogos**!*
While some cities have beautiful fireworks shows, you're guaranteed to hear people setting off firecrackers all month long no matter where you are.

Can we taste the passion fruit **liqueur**?
*Podemos experimentar o **licor** de maracujá?*
These are liqueurs made with *cachaça* and local fruits that have been fermenting since the previous year's Festa de São João. It's really strong and *realllly* sweet.

Teach me how to **square dance.**
*Me ensina a **dançar quadrilha**.*
This is some serious business. If you don't want to partake in the festivities, you can certainly watch the professionals at work. It's at the same level as Carnaval in some areas.

How much are the **tamales?**
*Quanto custam as **pamonhas?***
These are similar to Mexican dessert tamales.

I'd like a slice of **yucca cake,** please.
*Quero uma fatia de **bolo de aipim**, por favor.*

Music
Música

You just can't miss immersing yourself in the country's music. Music is so intertwined in Brazil's cultural fabric—there is no one *ritmo* in Brazil. There are hundreds that vary greatly depending on what region you find yourself in. Samba pulses through most of the country, but even this iconic style boasts many variations. Perhaps you've heard of *MPB* (Brazil's pop music) and *bossa nova* (Brazil's answer to jazz), but take a minute to examine other genres. From kids playing samba with makeshift instruments made from trashcans and buckets to the professionals strumming their *cavaquinhos* (small Brazilian guitars, similar to ukeleles) and tapping their *pandeiros* (tamborines), there's rhythm in every corner and every person.

Samba

We say samba, you say Brazil (and Carnaval and feathered headdresses and women clad in sparkly, dental-floss "clothes"...). Samba has it's variations from city to city, but if it were "one rhythm" to choose for Brazil as a whole, it's samba. Originally a traditional dance among African slaves, samba wasn't "sexy" (or widely known) until it arrived in Rio, where it transformed into what it is today—fast-paced and hot. Want a more traditional samba? Look for *samba de roda* or *samba recôncavo*. Like flashy costumes and fine women? It's *samba carioca* for you. Got a soft spot for jazz stylings? Try *samba partido alto*. There's also *samba reggae*, *samba com rap*, and *samba enredo*—a samba for all tastes is out there somewhere. **Popular artists:** Beth Carvalho, Zeca Pagodinho (*carioca*); Fundo de Quintal, Revelação, Délcio Luis (*partido alto*); Olodum, Ilê Aiyê (*samba reggae*); Marcelo D2, Rappin Hood (*samba com rap*).

MPB

MPB (*música popular brasileira*) puts a modern spin on classic Brazilian sounds. It's easy-listening rock without the smaltzy connotation. *MPB* is heard nationwide but more heavily in Rio and the south. **Popular artists:** Caetano Veloso, Gilberto Gil, Vanessa da Mata, Marisa Monte.

Bossa Nova

Influenced by American jazz, *bossa nova* is slow and calm with mellow lyrics. This is samba on tranquilizers. Originating in Rio, it is also mostly popular there and in the south. **Popular artists:** Tom Jobim, João Gilberto, Vinicius de Moraes.

Pagode Baiano

What do you get when you mix sirens and cell phone rings with a jammin' rhythm and hardcore lyrics? Upbeat party music, or *pagode*. When the amps are full blast, expect to see lots of people dancing like they're dry humping the air. These tunes are unique to Salvador and mostly appreciated by Bahian youth. **Popular artists:** Psirico, Parangolé.

Axé

Translated as "good energy," *axé* is movement-inducing happy percussion music best experienced live. The singers feed off the audience's energy and vice versa. You can't stand still for *axé*, and if you've got two left feet, just jump. If you're in Salvador for Carnaval, you'll definitely hear *axé* music. **Popular artists**: Ivete Sangalo, Timbalada, Chiclete com Banana.

Forró

A cross between the freaking you did in middle school and square dancing, *forró* is like polka music with a Latin flair. You can't escape the sounds of *forró* during June in northeast Brazil, where it's the official music of the region's Festas Juninas. In some cities it's even prohibited to play any other rhythm during this time. But the music isn't limited to June or the northeast—*forró* is loved year-round all over the country. **Popular artists**: Luiz Gonzaga, Dominguinhos, Adelmario Coelho, Flávio José.

Funk Carioca

A rhythm straight from the *favelas* of Rio, *funk* is popular all over Brazil. Get your freak on at a *baile funk*, because this music is bumpin'. **Popular artists**: Bochecha, MC Sapão.

Frevo

Frevo is Recife's main contribution to the music scene. With mainly brass band instruments leading the way, it's got an upbeat sound that will make you move your feet so fast it can make water boil! That's at least the theory of where the name came from (from *ferver* "to boil"). *Frevo* is the music of Recife's carnival and the dance is just as exciting as the music itself. Men and women acrobatically dance with tiny umbrellas and colorful props... it's something you can't miss if you are in Pernambuco. It's not the type of music you listen to on your MP3, so there aren't really any popular artists.

Maracatu

Another of Recife's signature rhthyms, *maracatu* has a rich African-Brazilian history and is almost exclusively accompanied by a folkloric dance. It's predominately percussion instruments playing a methodic beat. Mostly heard in Pernambuco, you will always see it in parades and street parties throughout Recife and the rest of the state. Along with *frevo*, it shares a special place in every *pernambucano*'s heart. Like *frevo*, there aren't any famous names in *maracatu*.

Arrocha

Bahia's answer to cheesy tunes. This music will have you singing along to the repetitive lyrics as you slow dance with that special someone. **Popular artists**: Silvano Salles, Pablo.

Sertanejo

Cowboys come out to play. The Brazilian equivalent of country-western, complete with funny hats, tight jeans, and cowboy boots. Popular in Goiás. **Popular artists**: Gustavo Lima, Luan Santana, Zezé de Camargo e Luciano, Chitãozinho e Xororó.

Rock

Not much to be said here, as Brazilian rock is heavily influenced by America's rock scene. *Rock* is mostly popular in the south. **Popular artists**: Cássia Eller.

★★★ Going Home
Indo pra Casa

After an entire day's worth of partying, you'll be ready for an air-conditioned hotel room. If you're partying far from your place, make sure to grab a cab. Even if every local you've met so far has been friendly and nice, there are plenty of people looking to take advantage of you and they'll usually come out at night.

Damn! It's so late. **Let's get outta here.**
*Caralho! É tarde demais. **Vamos embora.***

Party's over. Let's go back to the hotel.
Já era. Vamos pro hotel.

Let's bounce.
Bora.

Angela is **passed out.** We should take her home.
*Angela tá **desmaida**. Vamos levar ela pra casa.*

I'm tired and wanna go home.
***Tô cansado/a** e quero ir pra casa.*

We should grab a taxi.
Vamos pegar um taxi.
Again, be smart. You're a really easy target for a late night mugging.

I forgot where my hotel is. Can I crash at your place?
Esqueci onde é o meu hotel. Posso dormir na sua casa?

★★★ The Morning After
Na Manhã Seguinte

Did you have fun last night?
Você curtiu ontem à noite?

I had a blast.
Curti de montão. | Curti à vera.

I had a great time.
Me diverti muito.

It was great.
Foi ótimo.

It was cool.
Foi legal. | *maneiro.* | *bacana.* | *massa.*

It was awesome.
Foi show de bola.
Literally, "It was a ball show."

No, it was **shitty**.
*Não, foi ruim pra **cacete** | **porra**.*

I feel **awful**.
*Me sinto **péssimo**.*

I'm...
Tô...

> hungover.
> *de ressaca.*
>
> sick.
> *doente.*
>
> nauseous.
> *enjoado.*

going **to throw up**.
*com vontade de **vomitar**.*

I feel like **shit**.
*Tô me sentindo uma **merda**.*

I'm never drinking again.
Não vou beber nunca mais.

Let's sleep off our **hangover**s at the beach.
*Vamos curar a **ressaca** na praia.*

CHAPTER 6

Love Is in the Air
O Amor Está no Ar

After a day's worth of partying, you're either ready to crash hard or are looking to go home with a special someone. Hopefully for you, the party continues on to the bedroom. Brazil is known for its promiscuous culture, but don't expect the chase to be easy. You'll have to work for your reward. Brazilian men tend to be relentless when it comes to hitting on girls so step your game up and match them with your own original charm. If you do score a hottie, she's probably expecting you to take her back to your place. If you need some privacy, there are plenty of motels around that can accommodate a cheap one-nighter (more on motels on page 111).

★★★ Flirting
Flertando

Start with the basics. A compliment never hurt anybody.

Hello beautiful.
Oi linda.

You are...
Você é...

All in the Talk
Falando nisso

Go **flirt** with that hot chick at the bar.
*Vai **azarar** aquela gostosa no bar.*

I already tried **hitting on** her.
*Já tentei **dar em cima** dela.*

She's such a flirt.
Ela dá mole pros caras!
Watch out, she is all talk.

Don't even try for her. She only dates soccer players.
Nem tenta com ela. Ela é Maria-Chuteira.
Chuteira means "soccer cleat." She can also be *Maria Tatami* – someone who only dates guys who do Brazilian jiu-jitsu.

Daniel is desperately trying **pick up** that girl in the booty shorts.
*Danilo tá tentando **pegar** aquela garota de shortinho.*

I think he has a **crush on** me.
Acho que ele tá na minha.

He's definitely into me.
Ele tá a fim de mim.

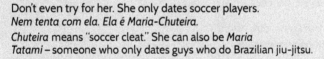

He/She is...
Ele/Ela é...

>cute.
>*bonitinho/a.*
>Can also be used for someone who is ugly but dresses well.

>adorable.
>*fofo/a.*

>handsome/pretty.
>*bonito/a.*

>beautiful.
>*lindo/a.*

>gorgeous.
>*lindíssimo/a.*
>If you add *íssimo/a* to the end of any adjective it's just like super-sizing the word.

>hot.
>*gostoso/a.*
>Literally, "tasty."

>sexy.
>*sexy.*

Can I have your number?
Me dá seu telefone?

Do you come here often?
Você vem sempre aqui?

Have we met before?
A gente já se conhece?

Can I buy you a drink?
Posso te pagar uma bebida?

Wanna dance?
Quer dançar?

Can I kiss you?
Posso beijar você?

You wanna hook up?
Quer ficar comigo?

Let's...
Vamos...

> take a walk.
> *dar um rolé.*
>
> go to the movies.
> *ao cinema.*
>
> go back to my place.
> *pra minha casa.*

I want to spend the night with you tonight.
Quero dormir com você hoje.

★★★ Body
Corpo

Body image is not taken lightly in Brazil. With the bikini beach culture, everyone goes to the gym and everyone works for what they've got. For girls it's about thick legs and a tight butt. For guys it's big biceps and a chiseled six-pack. *Brasileiros* take care of their bodies and dress well because other people notice and will judge. What better way to tell someone that you're interested than to show them you noticed. And, unlike in the Western world, where a shade above anorexic is sexy, Brazilians like some meat on their bones. Curves, muscles, booty—skinny isn't sexy here.

You've got...
Você tem...

> a bangin' body.
> *um corpaço.* | *um corpo maneiro.*

> a nice figure.
> *um shape legal.*

> beautiful eyes.
> *um belo par de olhos.* | *olhos bonitos.*

★★★ Terms of Endearment
Palavras de Carinho

An easy way to get intimate is to use diminutives in your speech. These are generally formed by adding the suffixes *-inho* and *-inha* to nouns, adjectives, and names. So the word *fofa* or "cutie," becomes *fofinha* (an extra-cute cutie). You can also do the opposite using augmentatives, which can also express intimacy, but an indication of respect is thrown in the mix. For example, *bonitona* which would literally be "big beauty."

Darling
Querido/a

Rate Your Mate
Escolhendo a Dedo

He's...
Ele é...

a hottie.
um gato.

a 10.
um pão.

really built.
malhado. | sarado.

She's...
Ela é...

a hottie.
uma gata.

nice legs.
pernuda.
Literally, "nice-legged."

a fine piece of meat.
um filé.

a 10.
um pitel.

a MILF.
uma coroa gostosa.

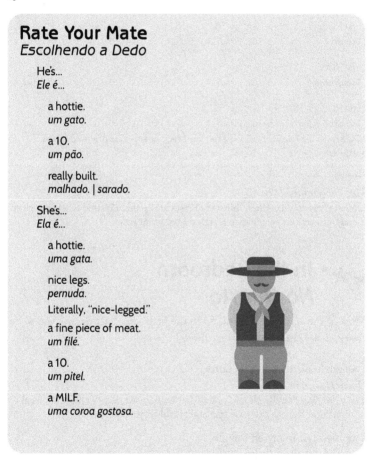

Sweetheart
Coração

Pumpkin
Meu bem
Literally, "my welfare."

Cutie
Fofo/a

(My) love
(Meu) amor

Honey
Docinho | Meu/minha nego/a
Meu nego/minha nega literally means "my black boy/girl" and is used in the northeast.

Sweetie
Meu filho/minha filha
Literally, "my son/daughter." But the phrases are commonly used to address close friends, or between people with a high degree of intimacy.

★★★ In the Bedroom
No Quarto

Most of the activities you will do in the bedroom don't require you to be very verbal. It never hurts to try though.

I wanna **hook up** with that hottie.
Quero ficar com aquele/a.
The word *ficar* literally means "to stay" but is also used in the context of casual relationships. You can call your late-night "buddy" your *ficante*.

I want you all to myself tonight.
Quero você só pra mim hoje.

Not So Terms of Endearment
Termos Não Tão Carinhosos

If you need to call someone out, try some of these words.

loser
zero à esquerda

Joe Schmoe
Zé Ninguém

hoochie
piriguete

slut
piranha

ugly woman
canhão

cougar
perua
Literally, "turkey." Often used to describe a very flashy woman – she doesn't necessarily have to be older.

whore
vagabunda

trust-fund baby/socialite
mauricinho (male) / *patricinha* (female)

playboy
playboy

player
pica de mel

pimp
farpado
Literally, "barbwire fence."

When you kiss me like that it turns me on.
Quando você me beija assim me dá muito tesão.

Tell me how you like it.
Me fala como você gosta.

Take off your clothes.
Tira a sua roupa.

Let's...
Vamos...

> have sex.
> *transar. | fazer sexo. | fazer amor.*

> fuck
> *foder. | trepar.*
> You can also use the verb *comer* to say "hit that," as in "I'd like to hit that"
> (*Queria comer ela*).

> have a quickie.
> *dar uma rapidinha.*

> I'm very excited.
> *Estou muito exitado/a.*

I want it...
Quero...

> faster.
> *mais rápido.*

> slower.
> *mais devagar.*

> deeper.
> *mais fundo.*

> harder.
> *mais forte.*

Like this?
Assim?

Are you wet?
Tá molhadinha?

Do you want me to finger you?
Quer uma siririca?

Do you like it?
Você gosta?

It feels so good.
Tá gostoso.

Don't stop.
Não pare.

Are you coming?
Tá gozando?

I'm gonna cum!
Vou gozar!

Was it good for you?
Foi bom pra você?

★★★ Motels
Motéis

Don't be fooled when you see the Vegas-style neon flashing lights of the motel signs all around the cities. A motel in Brazil isn't your standard Ramada Inn; it's explicitly designed as a rendezvous point for one-night stands and booty calls. Brazil is a predominately Catholic country, and it's not unusual for people to live with their parents before they get married, so these motels are common meet-up stations for couples—no shame involved.

Rooms rent by the hour or night, and standard units come with mirrored ceilings and walls, a set of extra sheets, and a TV full of free porn. You can get upgraded rooms (with an erotic chair or a jacuzzi bathtub), but you'll pay more. Forgot your edible panties or condoms? Don't worry, you can buy it at the motel, along with some other kinky trinkets.

Can you bring up some fresh **sheets**?
*Você pode me trazer **lençóis** limpos?*

Should we do it in the **shower**?
*Vamos transar no **chuveiro**?*

How much is it **per hour**? I've got a lot of energy tonight.
*Quanto é **por hora**? Tô com muita energia hoje.*

I'd like a room with an **erotic chair**.
*Quero um quarto com **cadeira erótica**.*

Does the medieval suite come with chain-mail armor?
A suíte medieval vem com armadura?
Some motels have themed rooms: Egyptian, Japanese, Western, etc.

★★★ Body Parts
Partes do Corpo

Like in English, there's an endless list of words for female and male body parts. We're just skimming the surface here. Some of the translations listed below are not only vulgar but insulting, so we aren't recommending you use these directly with someone you might have a chance with, let alone feelings for.

Penis
Pênis
Some more vulgar translations are: *rola, pau, pica, cacete, pinto,* and *espada*.

Prostitution
Prostituição

Prostitution is technically legal in Brazil, although it is in no way glorified. Organizations have offered free English classes for prostitutes, so there may be a chance you'll be negotiating *em inglês*. In case you aren't, here are a few basics.

How much for...?
Quanto custa para...?

an hour
uma hora

a blow job
um boquete

a little anal
um pouco de anal

the whole night
a noite inteira

What can I get for 10 *reais*?
O que você faz por 10 reais?

Can you **lower** the price for me?
*Pode **abaixar** o preço pra mim?*

That's a **good price**.
*É um **bom preço**.*

Vagina
Vagina
The more vulgar translations are: *buceta, xereca, piriquita, perereca, xoxota,* and *bacalhau.*

Butt
Bumbum

Ass
Bunda | Traseiro | Rabo | Cadeiras

Little/Big butt
Popozinho/Popozão

Anus
Cú

Breasts
Peitos

Boobs
Air bags | Tetas | Melões | Chupetas | Seios | Mamas

Balls
Ovos | Bolas | Culhões | Bagos

Clitoris
Clitóris | Botão | Broto de feijão | Castanha | Dente-de-alho | Pinguelo | Dedo sem unha

★★★ Positions
Posições

Let's do it...
Vamos fazer...

> missionary style.
> *papai-mamãe.*
> With legs spread, it's called *frango assado* (roast chicken).
>
> doggy-style.
> *de quatro.*
>
> wheelbarrow
> *carrinho de mão*

cowgirl
coqueirinho

reverse cowgirl
escorpião

Wanna try... ?
Quer experimentar... ?

a threesome
sexo a três

an orgy
uma orgia | uma suruba

anal sex
sexo anal

69
meia-nove

finger banging
siririca

oral sex
sexo oral

★★★ Some Good Words to Know
Algumas Palavras pra Saber

The Verbs:

To suck/lick
Chupar

To grab
Segurar

To touch
Tocar

To cuddle
Ficar aconchegado

To kiss
Beijar

To slap
Bater (em)

To squeeze
Apertar

To dry hump
Esfregar(se)

To give head
Chupar manga | Tocar a flauta | Cantar no microfone

To eat pussy
Beijar a perereca | Dar uma linguadinha | Cair de boca no tapete | Lavar o carro por baixo

The Nouns:

Physical affection
Carinho
Someone who is *carinhoso* is a caring person.

Tickle
Cócegas
Fazer cócegas is to tickle someone.

Caress
Cafuné

Soft kiss
Selinho

Strong kiss (like a plunger)
Chupão

Foreplay
Preliminares

Blow job
Boquete | Chupeta

Condom
Camisinha | Capacete | Capote | Touca | Chapéu
Estourar means "to break," so if the condom breaks...it *estourou.*

The pill
A pílula
"To be on the pill" is "to take." *Eu tomo a pílula* (I'm on the pill).

CHAPTER 7

Time Out
Intervalo

Face it, when everything is said and done, you're going to be exhausted. Right now, it's time to decompress. You're in Brazil, so bring on the *preguiça baiana* (Bahian laziness).

★★★ At the Beach
Na Praia

The beach is the ultimate "rehab," a place to soak in all the cultural richness and beauty Brazil has to offer. It's where you go to see and be seen, to kick back and hang out with friends. If you're looking for some quiet, down time, this isn't the place. This "holy ground" is packed with bodies preening, sunning, playing volleyball, selling food, hawking trinkets...You name it, they've got it.

Let's go for **a dip**.
*Vamos dar **um mergulho**.*

I don't want **to swim** now.
Num tô a fim de **nadar** *agora.*

I just want to...
Só quero...

> sunbathe.
> *tomar sol.*
>
> get some color.
> *pegar uma cor.*
>
> get a tan.
> *pegar um bronze.*
>
> go for a stroll.
> *dar uma caminhada.*

Can you put some **sunscreen** on my back?
Passa **protetor** *nas minhas costas?*

Dos and Don'ts
Certo e Errado

Be social.

Own your body – show some skin.

Kick back and enjoy the view.

Don't bring a lot of stuff. That's what dorky *farofeiros* (people who lug the kitchen sink to the beach) do. Definitely not cool.

Keep an eye on your belongings or ask someone to watch out for them while you take a dip in the water.

Don't bring a lot of money. Bring small bills instead of R$100 or R$50 bills.

Don't go topless. Despite the tiny bikinis, nudity is still taboo in Brazil, and in most cities it's against the law.

Take it easy on the rays — your skin looks like beef jerky.
Cuidado com o sol — sua pele tá parecendo um maracujá.
Maracujá means "passion fruit," which has a shriveled rind.

That **Speedo** is tiny!
*Essa **sunga** é pequena!*

Who's that chick with the **bangin' bod**?
*Quem é aquela gata com aquele **corpaço**?*

Your **bikini**'s rad — where'd you get it?
*Seu **biquini** tá bem legal — onde você comprou?*

I want to get one of those **itsy-bitsy bikinis**.
*Quero comprar **um desses biquinis fio dental**.*
Fio dental literally means "dental floss."

Where's the nearest **beach bar**?
*Onde fica a **barraca** mais próxima?*

Can you keep an eye on my stuff?
Pode ficar de olho nas minhas coisas?

Nice **tan line**!
*Que **marca linda**! | **marquinha***
This is not sarcastic. In Brazil, the bigger and darker the tan line, the better. If you don't believe us, grab a Brazilian *Playboy* magazine and see for yourself.

Where's that guy selling the **sarongs**?
*Onde tá aquele cara vendendo as **cangas**?*
Don't even think about bringing a big ol' towel to the beach. A sarong will do just fine.

Snack
Lanche

Beach 101: Leave the cooler at home. Brazilian beaches are full of people selling ice cream, Popsicles, grilled shrimp, meat, fried fish, beer, water, soda, and pretty much anything you'd like (or wouldn't like) to eat or drink. Embrace the nonstop parade of food. Sit back, take in the scene, and indulge your cravings.

Let's have a **snack**.
*Vamos fazer um **lanche**.*

I feel like having...
Tô com vontade de comer...

> shrimp.
> *camarão.*
>
> a kebab.
> *um espetinho.*
>
> a Popsicle.
> *um picolé.*
>
> crab broth.
> *um caldo de sururú.*
> Nice and hot, brought to you in some dude's thermos!
>
> fish.
> *peixe.*
> Usually served fried (*frito*), but you can ask for it grilled (*grelhado*).
>
> salty snacks.
> *tira-gostos.*
>
> a sandwich.
> *um sanduíche.*
> You won't find a BLT or club—there's nothing too fancy here. The most common is *misto* (ham and cheese) or *natural* (chicken, lettuce, and carrots). They can be toasted (*quente*) or cold (*frio*).
>
> *grilled cheese.*
> *queijo coalho.*
> *Queijo coalho* is a salty, lightweight cheese that, when served at the beach, is browned over a hand-held charcoal oven and often sprinkled with oregano and/or garlic, and sometimes eaten with molasses.

cashews.
castanhas.
These come sweet, salty, natural, or spicy and go great with a *brisa* (beer).

oysters.
lambretas.
On a half shell, served with lime and hot sauce.

Fun in the sun
Pegando uma cor

There's so much going on at the beach already, but if you're one who has to keep moving, there are plenty of games and sports that are only played there.

Beach soccer
Futebol de areia
This is basically soccer played on sand, but with fewer players, a shorter game clock, and a smaller field.

Beach volleyball
Vôlei de praia | Futvolei
Brazilians love soccer so much they've created this game—it's volleyball, but you can't use your hands. You see this all over the beaches in Rio.

Rugby
Rugby

Badminton
Peteca
For the old folks on Sunday morning.

Paddle ball
Frescobol

Scuba diving
Mergulho

Surfing Etiquette
"Etiqueta" de Surf

Most surfing etiquette rules are common sense, but if you're in need of a refresher, here are a few pointers to help you avoid an uncomfortable situation mid-Atlantic.

Rule #1: Right of way	*Regra #1: Direito de onda*
Rule #2: Don't drop in	*Regra #2: Não "dropin"	"rabere"*
Rule #3: Paddle behind	*Regra #3: Rema pra fora*
Rule #4: Don't ditch your board	*Regra #4: Não largue a prancha*
Rule #5: Don't snake	*Regra #5: Rema à volta do break*

Oh, and if you mess up, a simple apology will suffice: *Desculpe, você está legal?*

Surfing
Surf

Windsurfing
Windsurf

Boogieboarding
Bodyboard

Kitesurfing
Kitesurfe

The waves are big today.
O mar tá gigante hoje.
Mar is literally, "ocean."

Can I rent a **board** here?
*Posso alugar uma **prancha** aqui?*

This guy doesn't know how to surf for shit.
Esse cara é o maior raule.

Did you **wax** my board?
*Você **passou parafina** na minha prancha?*

That surfer **paddled** out pretty far.
*Aquele surfista **remou** bem longe daqui.*

I finally **caught a wave!**
*Finalmente **peguei uma onda**!*

★★★ Shopping
Compras

There are three main shopping scenes: the mall, the marketplace, and the street, each with its own atmosphere, crowd, and style. If shopping isn't your thing, skip the mall and head straight for the markets. There you can find (or negotiate) the best deals for souvenirs that are actually worth buying.

At the mall
No shopping

Malls or *shoppings*, as they are called, are filled with stores ranging from high-end boutiques to more affordable chains and shops. As in most places, the character of the mall and its content are tailored to its audience. This means that the nicer the neighborhood, the fancier the mall (and the pricier the shops). Some malls are an overwhelming consumer maze. The trick to survival is to let go. Since you probably don't really know where you're going, any path will take you there. No need to stress; you'll find your way out eventually. Plus, all malls have a food court area, and the larger ones usually also have a movie theater and a supermarket. Oh, and did we mention they're air-conditioned? Yep, they're great escapes from the scorching sun.

30 %
promação

Let's go to the **mall**.
*Vamos pro **shopping***.

Women love to go **window shopping**.
*Mulher adora **bater perna***.

She is so **posh**. She only likes **designer clothes**.
*Ela é **chique** demais. Só gosta de **roupa de grife***.

I'm all about **name brands**.
*Só visto **roupa de marca***.

Look at that **display**! That outfit is killer.
*Olha essa **vitrine**! Essa roupa é demais.*

I want to check out that **store**.
*Quero dar uma olhada nessa **loja**.*

Let's go inside.
Vamos entrar.

Everything is super **cheap/expensive**.
*Tudo é super **barato/caro**.*

It's **on sale**.
*Está **em promoção**.*

What do you think about this?
O que você acha disto?

It's pretty, right?
É lindo, né?
I can't decide if I should get it.
Não sei se deveria comprar.

It's such a good sale that I can't help myself.
A promoção é tão boa que não consigo resistir.

I'm going **to buy** it.
*Vou **comprar**.*

You're going to buy all that?
Você vai comprar tudo isso?

I wanted to buy more.
Eu queria até comprar mais.

I won't **take long**. Just going to buy a few things.
*Não vou **demorar**. Só vou comprar umas coisinhas.*

The Movie Theater
O Cinema

Unless you're at a small or independent movie theater, it should be relatively easy to see a film in English (a welcome relief if your head is fogged from all the Portuguese shouting going on around you). Hollywood blockbusters are usually shown in both their original version and dubbed in Portuguese, so make sure to double-check showtimes and hope there's no "D" for *dublado* (dubbed) under the movie title.

Want to watch a **movie**?
*Quer assistir um **filme**?*

What movie are they **playing**?
*Qual filme tá **passando**?*

Let's **see** the Brazilian one.
*Vamos **assistir** o filme brasileiro.*

No, I want to see an **action** flick.
*Não, quero assistir um filme **de ação**.*

Come on! It's in English with Portuguese **subtitles**.
*Vamos lá! É em inglês com **legendas** em português.*

Two **tickets** for the Meirelles movie, please.
*Dois **ingressos** para o filme Meirelles, por favor.*

Do you want **popcorn**?
*Você quer **pipoca**?*

Of course. It's **free** here!
*Claro. É **grátis** aqui!*
Depending on the theater, you may score a bag of popcorn.

Should we take a **break**?
*Vamos fazer uma **pausa**?*

The **food court** is right over there.
*A **praça de alimentação** é aqui perto.*

Money
Dinheiro

Need it or want it? Toe-*may*-to, toe-*mah*-to. If you find something you like, don't overthink it, just get it. Unless you can't actually afford it, in which case we strongly encourage you to stick with window shopping.

How much does this cost?
Quanto custa?

That's too **expensive**.
*Tá muito **caro**.*

That's a **bargain**.
*É uma **pechincha**.*

I'll take it.
Vou levar.

Can I pay with...?
Posso pagar com...?

> credit card
> *cartão de crédito*
>
> debit card
> *cartão de débito*
>
> cash
> *dinheiro*
>
> check
> *cheque*

I'd like to pay in full.
Quero fazer um pagamento à vista.
Sometimes you might get a discounted price if you pay in full in cash.

I need to pay in **installments**.
*Preciso pagar a **prestação**.*

Is it possible to buy **on credit**?
*Posso comprar a **crédito**?*

Do you have **change** for a fifty?
*Tem **troco** pra cinquenta?*

I don't have a smaller **bill**.
*Não tenho uma **nota** menor.*

At the marketplace
Na feira

If you're after cheap buys and aren't afraid to negotiate, make sure to check out a few local markets. Some indoor venues are set up specifically for bargaining down the price of goods, while others are open-air markets that pop up around town (think high-end flea markets). Have cash handy to ensure you're able to make all of your purchases, especially in the smaller markets. But don't draw attention to yourself by pulling out a wad of bills — play it smart and low-key when you reach for your money. Remember, you're not at the mall; there are no security cameras here to deter crime.

Do you want to go to the **market** today?
*Quer ir ao **mercado** hoje?*

They set up the **open-air market** really early this morning.
*Montaram a **feira livre** bem cedo essa manhã.*

I just went by a **small arts and crafts fair** in the plaza.
*Acabei de passar por uma **feirinha de artesanato** lá na praça.*

We can go if you want to.
Podemos ir se você quiser.

Look what I found!
Olha o que descobri!

What's that over there?
O que é aquilo lá?

This is amazing!
É incrível!

Can I try it on?
Posso experimentar?

Do you have another one like it?
Tem outro como esse?

Do you make this yourself?
É você quem faz?

I've never seen anything like it.
Nunca vi nada parecido.

I like that one.
Gostei desse.

No. I prefer the other one more.
Não. Eu prefiro o outro.

On the street
Na rua

You're a tourist and you stand out like a tourist, so some locals will try to rip you off. That's just the way it's going to be. There are street vendors all around. Don't let anyone put a necklace on you or tie anything to your wrist—it's a pain trying to politely tell someone that you don't want their low-quality jewelry. If you actually do want to make a purchase, be savvy. Haggle away but don't let your guard down.

How much is this?
Quanto é?

Can I have it **for less**?
*Pode fazer **mais barato**?*

That's way too expensive.
Tá caro pra caramba.

How much will you give it to me for?
Por quanto você faz?

Can't you give me a better price?
Pode fazer mais barato pra mim?

What if I buy more than one?
E se eu comprar mais de um?

Let me think about it.
Deixa eu pensar.

I'm not sure.
Não sei.

I haven't decided yet.
Ainda não decidi.

You're totally ripping me off.
Ai você tá me roubando.

Can't do it.
Assim não dá.

I'm not going to buy anything.
Não vou comprar nada.

★★★ Food
Comida

Like the people, Brazilian food is full of color, flavor, and spice. Whether at home or at a restaurant, a meal is a sacred time where food is meant to be enjoyed. Although it's easy to score some food fast—there are food stands and restaurants everywhere—it won't be fast food. As a rule, Brazilians don't eat while walking down the street, driving, taking the subway, or riding the bus. It's simply considered rude. If you want to blend in with the local diners, then sit down, take a load off, and savor your tasty treat.

You hungry?
Tá com fome?

Hell yeah, I'm hungry.
Tô com uma fome danada.

I'm starving.
Tô caindo de fome. | *Tô morrendo de fome.*

I'm so famished I could eat **a horse**.
*Tô com tanta fome, que seria capaz de comer **um boi**.*
Boi is literally "bull."

I'm so hungry I'm about to pass out.
Tô desmaiando de fome.

I'm jonesing for some...food.
Tô a fim de uma comida...

> American
> *americana*
> Don't ask for "American" food—nobody will know what you're talking about. Just ask where the nearest *lanchonete* (café) is. This is where you'll find cheeseburgers (*x-burgers*, pronounced "sheez-burger"), milkshakes (*milkshakes*), and fries (*batatas fritas*). Other typical sandwich offerings:

the *americano* with ham, cheese, egg, lettuce, tomato, and mayo; the hamburger, like an American burger but also made with bacon, ham, and eggs...the way a hamburger should be; and the *frango na chapa*, grilled chicken and ham.

Chinese
chinesa

Chinese food has been adapted to the South American palate, so a spring roll in Brazil is filled with cheese instead of vegetables. Yup, cheese, a food that's never used in real Chinese cooking. But hey, if you're into that, go ahead.

Italian
italiana

At least Brazilians got something somewhat right. Pasta and pizza—delish!

> There's not enough ketchup in this pasta.
> *Não tem ketchup suficiente nesse macarrão.*
> Wondering why the bottles of ketchup and mustard are on the table? Brazilians like to put it on their pizza or in their pasta. You can skip it if you want.

Japanese
japonesa

São Paulo is chock-full of Japanese-Brazilians who've managed to keep their food authentic. It's popular all over the country.

Middle Eastern
árabe

You'll mostly find Middle-Eastern food served in fast-food joints: Armenian pizza (their version of *lahmajoon*), *kibe* (made with beef instead of lamb), tabbouleh, and hummus.

I'm not hungry—I just scarfed down some *coxinhas*.
Estou sem fome—acabei de devorar umas coxinhas.

No, I just ate lunch.
Não, acabei de almoçar.

I've got the munchies.
Tô com larica.

Let's grub.
Vamos rangar.

Should we eat at that new Japanese joint?
Vamos comer naquele boteco japonês novo?

Did you **have breakfast** already?
*Você já **tomou café**?*

Do you want to **have dinner** with me tonight?
*Você quer **jantar** comigo hoje à noite?*

Let's grab a bite to eat before we hit the club.
Vamos fazer um lanche antes de ir pra boate.

Eating out
Comer fora

Lunch is the heaviest meal in Brazil, which means that for many, eating out happens at midday rather than in the evening. There's an infinite number of dining options to satisfy those cravings whether you're by yourself or with friends. When figuring out seating arrangements, it's common to hear people say: *Quem senta na ponta, paga a conta.* (Literally, "Who sits at the head of the table, pays the bill.") Don't worry about it. It's an ongoing joke that never gets old and is of little consequence. Just laugh along and enjoy your meal.

Let's go to...
Vamos pra...

> a restaurant.
> *um restaurante.*
>
> the farmer's market.
> *a feira.*
> A *feira* can also be described as a "street fair." Like in the United States, different neighborhoods host a farmer's market on different days of the week. *Feiras* feature the best fruits and vegetables at great prices. It's also

a wonderful place for breakfast, tasting local produce, and peeking into the local lifestyle. If you make it to one, be sure to try the *caldo de cana* (sugar cane juice) and a *pastel* (fried pastry with either a sweet or savory filling).

an all-you-can-eat place.
um rodízio.
This isn't the pork-out buffet you see all over the U.S.—*rodízio*-style dining means servers come around with trayfuls of food until you've hit your limit. Usually *rodízios* serve pizza and pasta or seafood and steak.

a steakhouse.
uma churrascaria.
The glorious *churrascaria* is like a good ol' Texas steakhouse with meat, meat, and meat on the menu. The roaming servers at the *rodízio*-style *churrascaria* carve succulent slices from giant skewered hunks of grilled beef tableside. An impressive buffet in the middle of the restaurant is filled with rice, beans, sushi, and every type of salad imaginable. When you've stuffed your face too much, flip over that little green card on your table to the red side so the server stops bringing you meat and comes over with the dessert tray.

a café.
uma lanchonete.
A café is a great place to grab a quick bite when you're out and about. The menu usually has fresh juice, *açaí na tigela* (frozen açaí berries blended into a thick paste and sprinkled with granola or other fruit like bananas), ham-and-cheese sandwiches, and baked treats.

a café. (in the cute French sense)
um café.
These exist for tourists, but you won't see too many people drinking tall lattes or iced Frappuccinos. Caffeine is usually plain old coffee and maybe espresso. But honestly, real Brazilians get their coffee fix at *lanchonetes* (where it's served in small plastic cups) or from old men selling the brew from street carts.

a fast-food restaurant.
um restaurante fast-food.
McDonald's is a delicacy here. No joke.

a food-by-the-kilo restaurant.
um restaurante de comida a quillo (kilo).
These buffet-style restaurants are like supermarket salad bars but with entrées and side dishes thrown in. You pay by the kilo (usually 15 to 25 *reais* per kilo). Get as much as you want, but remember, it's all on your dime. Don't lose your receipt, because the cost of a lost ticket is enough food to feed an elephant.

lunch plate.
prato feito/PF.
At most *comida a quillo* restaurants they offer a fixed-price plate that's usually your choice of meat with rice, beans, and salad. If you're hungry and want a lot of food for a good price, this is the way to go; it's generally cheaper than if you were to weigh the same plate of food.

Has the waiter taken your **order**?
*O moço já anotou o seu **pedido**?*

Can I see a **menu**, please?
*Me da um **cardápio**, por favor.*

This place is...
Esse lugar é...

expensive.
caro.

cheap.
barato.

Waiter, could you please bring me the **bill**?
*Moço, pode trazer a **conta** por favor?*

I want to **close the tab**.
*Quero **fechar a conta**.*

I'm broke, I can't leave a **tip**.
*Tô duro, não posso dar **gorjeta**.*
Your server doesn't expect a tip—it's totally optional.

Bon appétit!
Bom apetite!

Yum!!!
Hummmm!!!!

The best way to let someone know you like their food is to tell them. No need to be shy. We all like compliments.

Delicious.
Delicioso.

Tasty.
Gostoso.

Delish.
Uma delícia.

I want more.
Quero mais.

Just a little bit more.
Só mais um pouquinho.

Loved it!
Amei!

I'm satisfied.
Tô satisfeito.
It's more polite to use this expression when declining food rather than *Tô cheio* (I'm full); saying you're full can be considered rude.

After I ate that *feijoada*, I had a food coma.
Depois de comer aquela feijoada, eu apaguei.

Nasty
Desagradável

As adventurous as you think you are with food, there will be something that'll churn your stomach.

That food's disgusting—I can't even swallow it!
Esse rango tá nojento—Não desce!

Jesus, are you going to eat that? Gross!
Meu Deus, você vai comer isso? Que nojo!

Yuck!
Argh!

The food was...
A comida tava...

> crap.
> *uma porcaria.*
>
> awful.
> *ruim.*
>
> too sweet.
> *muito doce.*
>
> too salty.
> *muito salgada.*
>
> too sour.
> *muito azeda.*
>
> spoiled.
> *estragada.*

Drinks
Bebidas

It's gonna be hot and you're gonna get thirsty. Don't be too predictable. There are other things besides beer, you know.

I'm...
Tô...

> thirsty.
> *com sede.*
>
> parched.
> *morto de sede.*
>
> dehydrated.
> *desidratado.*

Can I have a glass of water?
Eu quero um copo d'água.
It may seem rude, but when you're asking for something, you usually just say, "I want" instead of "Can I have?"

My girlfriend only drinks **sparkling water,** but I prefer **still.**
*Minha namorada só bebe **água com gás**, mas eu prefiro **água sem gás**.*

I got the runs for a week after I drank **tap water.**
*Tive diarréia por uma semana depois que tomei **água da torneira**.*

Don't give me **room-temp water** — I want it nice and **cold.**
*Não me de **água natural** — eu quero bem **gelada**.*

Coconut water's the jam!
Água de coco é legal!
Best when fresh out of a green coconut — usually how it's served on the beach, on the street, or at a *lanchonete.* But you can also buy this tropical treat in stores (bottled or boxed). Oh, and careful with the pronunciation: "CO-co" (accent on the first syllable) means "coconut"; "co-CÔ" (accent on the last syllable) means "shit." I mean, unless you want shitty water.

Sugarcane juice
Caldo de cana

I want...juice.
Quero suco de...

> guava
> *goiaba*

lime
limão

mango
manga

orange
laranja

passion fruit
maracujá

pineapple
abacaxi

Local fruits
Frutas locais

Some tropical fruits never make it north of the equator. If you see
something at the market or on the menu you've never tasted before,
don't be a sissy – try it.

Siriguela: This is similar in look and flavor to a kumquat.

Cupuaçu: Related to the *cacao* fruit, *cupuaçu* is usually served in juice
form.

Graviola: Soursops have a spiny exterior; the custardy flesh is tart.

Jaca: The jackfruit is not as stinky as its cousin, the durian, but it
certainly is pungent.

Umbú: This small Brazilian plum is green and tart.

Acerola: The Barbados or West Indian cherry isn't native to Brazil but
thrives in the climate. Another tart fruit that's super high in vitamin C.

Açaí: A berry a little smaller than a blueberry. This fruit is known as a
natural energy booster. You'll see it as ice cream, juice, blended with
other fruit, then topped with tapioca or granola.

Avocado smoothie
Vitamina de abacate
An avocado smoothie may sound weird, but don't dis it till you've tried it. Mixed with milk and sugar, this super-popular choice plays to the avocado's true nature (it is, after all, a fruit). If you aren't adventurous, you can opt for a smoothie from more familiar additions like bananas (*bananas*) or papayas (*mamões*).

Coffee
Café

> black
> *preto*

> decaf
> *descafeinado*

> with or without...?
> *com ou sem...?*

> > milk
> > *leite*

> > sugar
> > *açúcar*

> > sweetener
> > *adoçante*

Cup of coffee
Xícara de café

Small coffee
Cafezinho

Tea
Chá

Soda
Refrigerante
Brazil's favorite soft drink is *guaraná*, and Guaraná Antártica is the most popular brand.

> regular
> *normal*

diet
zero | light | diet

Traditional Brazilian dishes
Pratos brasileiros tradicionais

Lip-smacking, melt-in-your-mouth food—that's Brazilian cuisine. Hope you like beans and rice (*feijão com arroz*) because that, along with the occasional salad (*salada*), comes with just about every meal. There are tons of options and you should try them all. Here are a few suggestions.

Feijoada
A salted-pork and black bean stew served with rice...and other things.

Muqueca
Seafood stew. *Muqueca capixaba*, influenced by Native Brazilian cuisine, is cooked in a traditional clay pot and can be made with fish, shrimp, crab, or lobster. In the northeast, *muqueca baiana* takes on African touches with the addition of coconut milk and palm oil (*dendê*), which gives this stew a distinctive yellow tint. Served with *farinha* (manioc flour), rice, salad, and sometimes black-eyed peas.

Tutú à mineira
A paste of beans and manioc flour. Very popular in Minas Gerais.

Vaca atolada
Literally, "mud-stranded cow." Sounds a little gross, but it's a popular meat and cassava stew typical of *caipira* cuisine from the interior of the state of São Paulo.

Arroz carreteiro
Typical of Rio Grande do Sul, this rice dish is mixed with meat and spices.

Bobó de camarão
This northeastern dish is made with a cooked cassava paste, palm oil, spices, and shrimp.

Escondidinho
The name of this dish means "hidden," which refers to the *carne de sol* (salty dry beef) that's hidden beneath a layer of cassava purée and served with lots of *pimenta* (hot sauce).

Feijão tropeiro
Pinto beans mixed with manioc flour, sausage, bacon, eggs, onions, and spices.
It's served with meat and rice.

Empadão goiano
This is the chicken potpie of Goiás, a state in central Brazil; it can also be made
with sausage or corn.

Bacalhau
Salted codfish. *Bacalhau* is very popular in Brazil because of the Portuguese
influence. It's cooked many ways, but the most common preparation is baked
with various spices.

Street food
Comida na rua

You'll never go hungry in Brazil—every other inch of dirt or pavement
sports a food cart. But don't expect diet-conscious preparations—just
enjoy the oh-so-yummy fat.

Acarajé
Peeled black-eyed peas formed into a ball and deep-fried in palm oil, then split
in half and stuffed with *vatapá* (spicy peanut, shrimp, and palm oil paste), *carurú*
(a cooked okra mush), and tomato salad. You'll find this mostly in Salvador.

Bolinhos de chuva
Every country has a version of sweet fried dough. This is Brazil's.

Bolinhos de bacalhau
Salt-cod fritters

Cocada
Sugar-coated grated coconut
Cocada queimada (or *cocada puxa-puxa*) is a chewier version made with brown
sugar. *Cocada branca* is made with condensed milk, so it's whiteish instead of
brownish.

Coxinha
Similar to a chicken croquette, but the shape resembles a chicken drumstick. The
name literally means "little thigh."

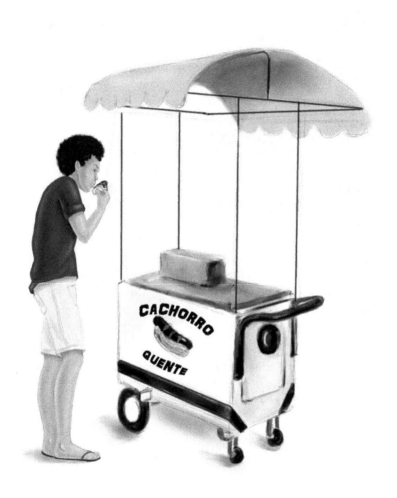

Cachorro quente
Hot dog. Go tame and top with ketchup and mustard, or go local and add peas, corn, fried shoestring potatoes, and tomato sauce.

Churrasco de gato
Meat on a stick.

Empadinha
Mini potpie filled with shrimp, chicken, or beef.

Kibe
Kibbeh, a savory deep-fried combination of wheat, beef (instead of the usual lamb), mint, and peanuts.

Mingau
Sweet breakfast porridge made with tapioca, corn, or oatmeal.

Milho cozido
Corn on the cob. If you want salt and butter, order *com sal e manteiga*.

Pamonha
A paste made from corn and milk that's boiled and wrapped in corn husks. It can be salty or sweet, and can be filled with cheese, sausage, or peppers.

Pão de queijo
Baked cheese balls.

Pastel
A crisp, fried pastry filled with sweet (*doce*) or savory (*salgado*) ingredients like guava jelly and cheese, banana, chocolate, coconut, meat, and cheese.

Pipoca
Popcorn comes either salted (*salgada*) or sweet (*doce*).

Beijú
Made with tapioca starch, this tortilla-like, flat cake is folded over and filled with the same kinds of stuff you see in *pastéis*.

Sweets
Doces

Always leave room for dessert. Can you say "delicious"?

Candy
Doce

Brigadeiro
Sort of like a truffle, this candy is made with chocolate, condensed milk, butter, and cocoa powder, then topped with sprinkles.

Beijinho
Like *brigadeiro*, but made with coconut instead of chocolate.

Romeo e Julieta
Slices of *queijo de Minas* (soft, mild white cheese) and *goiabada* (guava paste) eaten together.

Cake
Bolo
Cake is what's for breakfast in Brazil. It's not the gooey, frosting-coated type, but it's got a wide variety of flavors. Some of the more unique ones are *fubá* (a type of corn), *aipim* (yucca), *tapioca* (tapioca), and *banana* (banana).

Tart/Cake
Torta
This is any sort of elaborate cake with frosting or layers. It can also be a tart.

Mousse
Mousse
Mousses come in various fruit flavors, but the *mousse de maracujá* (passion fruit mousse) is the best.

Coconut custard
Quindim
A gelatinous treat made with eggs, sugar, and grated coconut.

Cookie
Biscoito
In every supermarket, corner store, or gas station there is a wall full of cookies. They range from wafers to Oreo sandwich–style to shortbread. Crackers are also called *biscoito salgado* (salty) when they're savory.

Ice cream
Sorvete

Peanut brittle
Pé de moleque

Trifle
Pavé

Flan
Pudim

ARTWORK CREDITS

page 13 map © Serban Bogdan/shutterstock.com

pages 1, 6, 25, 38, 55, 63, 79, 84, 89, 102, 103, 107, 109, 113, 118, 127 © Marish/shutterstock.com

pages 31, 46, 53, 105, 125, 136, 145 © Tatiana Minina

pages 73–78 stadiums © Valentin Ramon

ACKNOWLEDGMENTS

In the universe of people helping making this book happen, we would like to thank our editor Claire Chun for her patience with us and her ease in turning our scattered words into a coherent book. Thank you to Tatiana Minina for your beautiful illustrations. Thank you to Alex Beijos, Mirian Hong, David Gilbert, and Zarah Rahman for their contributions.

Alice: Thank you Beans—if it weren't for your Brazilian radio show on Saturdays at 2 in the morning and your *forró* sandwiches, I would never have taken the paths in life that I did. Thank you for your continual enthusiasm and indispensable friendship.

Nati: Thank you to Mi for all your shared wisdom about life, Portuguese language, and *brasilidade*. Thank you also to Champ for teaming up with me all those years ago for soccer Sundays.

Jadson: Above all, I would like to mention the Esporte Clube Bahia fans who made my heart beat faster each time I went to the stadium, showing me what true love means—it was definitely my first one. BBMP!!!!!!

ABOUT THE AUTHORS

Alice Rose is a former editor turned physical therapist and capoeira teacher in the Bay Area. She is a movement fanatic and when not teaching people how to move, you can find her hiking with her dog or scooting with her kids. She loves Brazilian music and food, and visits Bahia frequently with her family, including coauthor and husband, Jadson.

Nati Vale is an educator and writer with a PhD in Latin American literature. She fell in love with Portuguese in 2006 and is still head over heels, having spent time studying, traveling, and playing capoeira in Brazil and Portugal. If you can't find her on campus, she's probably out riding her bike, swimming at the pool, or hiding behind a book.

Born in Bahia, Brazil, **Jadson Caçador** has been living, teaching, and helping to raise awareness about Brazilian culture in the Bay Area for over a decade. Jadson's passions are playing in the sun with his kids, teaching capoeira, and eating acaraje (in no specific order).